No Other Medicine, but Hope

MEMOIRS OF A MINISTER'S WIFE

Marguerite McDaid

BLACKWATER PRESS

Editor
Antoinette Walker

Design & Layout
Paula Byrne

Cover Design
Melanie Gradtke

© Marguerite McDaid, 2002

ISBN 1 84131 580 X

Cover photograph courtesy of Siobhán Hegarty Photography, Letterkenny, Co. Donegal.

Produced in Ireland by Blackwater Press, Hibernian Industrial Estate, Greenhills Road, Tallaght, Dublin 24.

Contents

Acknowledgements

In writing this memoir, I owe my greatest thanks to my wonderful daughter Nicola, my best friend and confidant. She is the daughter that every parent would be proud to have. It is she who holds us all together.

My thanks also go to my wonderful friend, Majella Leonard. She is the friend who never fell by the wayside, the friend who dried my tears and above all, made me laugh when times were tough. A thousand thanks.

And finally my sons, son-in-law, and especially my three little grandsons, Cameron Cook, Jack McDaid and Dominic Cook, I thank you boys for your smiling little faces, which show me that life is definitely worth living, and every minute with you is precious.

for Luke

my raison d'être

1

London 1968

The best summer of my life, ever. I was eighteen-years-old, and away from home for the first time on my own. I was living in a dingy flat in Croydon with a few of the girls. The 'flat' consisted of one room with a smelly mattress on the bed, where the previous tenants or possibly their kids must have peed every night for years. The dark grimy bathroom was down two flights of stairs and shared by six other tenants. Our 'kitchen' was a sink and a small cooker in one corner of our room. But it was heaven. It was ours and no one could tell us when we could come and go.

Two weeks earlier as we wandered along the prom in Salthill, killing time and not appreciating the beauty and tranquillity of Galway Bay, we had mused over what to do for the summer. We had just finished our first-year university exams the previous week and we were free as the birds. But we had neither jobs nor money, so the summer ahead was looking very long and boring.

"We should really go to London for the summer, shouldn't we, and look for jobs there?" said one.

The rest of us looked at her as though she had lost her marbles.

"Not a chance," I laughed.

"We'd never be allowed. I know my father would have a fit if I asked," I added.

But that tiny seed had been sown in our minds, and with careful and precisely timed watering over the following few days, who knew what would happen.

Where would you stay? Who would look after you? You won't eat properly. What if you get sick? But they had to admit we were growing up. And they had to show they trusted us, so with great delight, three of us got the go ahead. We could hardly believe our luck.

Naturally, permission came with a giant handbook of do's and don'ts. Don't talk to strange men. Don't go out late at night. Don't be tempted to drink any 'funny' drinks. The list of promises we made read like the New York telephone directory. But what harm. We were on our way. And after all, what, if anything, did parents know about the world?

Full of expectation, we booked our flights from Dublin to Heathrow. We had a brilliant going-away party the night before we left. A bit like the American wake during the famine. Except we weren't going that far. But for our parents, it might as well have been to Australia.

Once there, the first few nights we stayed with newly married friends, but then it got a bit crowded. That was when we got our own abode, with the aforementioned smelly bed. God, I can still smell it when I think of it now. We spent the days looking for work and the nights partying. Within a week, we had all got jobs in various offices during the day, and in a local laundry from 5 to 8 pm five evenings a week. We worked like slaves in that laundry, dragging wet sheets out of boiling vats, loading them into giant dryers, then passing them through enormously hot rotation pressers, with steam hissing everywhere. We sweated like bulls in the intense moist heat. It must have been good for our complexions but we didn't think of that. A large colourfully attired African lady watched over us like a gaoler, to make sure we never rested. We got five shillings a week for it. Five nights at a shilling a night. Slave labour.

After three weeks of toil and play, word arrived through the Celtic grapevine that an Irish pub in London was looking for bar staff. One of our friends already worked there and the job included accommodation. So one quick interview that afternoon, and we were in. We dashed back to Croydon that night, packed our bags, said good riddance to our humble abode and the laundry, and moved in. No notice to the landlord was expected in those far off days.

So there we were. We had landed on our feet. Notting Hill Gate. The Hoop Bar and Mr Lynch's Irish Eating House Restaurant. Right on the corner beside the Tube station. Three young and innocent Irish barmaids in short black miniskirts with clinging white tops. The punters loved us. We loved the punters. The landlord was Irish and looked after us well, with accommodation just above the pub.

There was no shortage of requests for our company from nice young men. However, my father's words 'Do not go out with any strangers' rang like a clarion call in my ears each time I turned down an invitation. Eventually, however, the three of us fell madly in love. My young man called Chris was from Co Antrim and employed as an ice-lolly maker by Wall's, the ice-cream giants. Night after night he would sit on his bar stool and gaze lovingly at me over the counter until closing time. Then he would take me for an Indian in the Taj Mahal in Holland Park. A real authentic British Indian restaurant. The strange aromas that assailed the nostrils on entering were breathtaking. Well, it was only 1968 and packets of 'Vesta' beef curry had only just arrived in the West of Ireland. He wanted to marry me there and then. He had no money, no flat, no prospects, but so what?

All around us the Beatles were singing 'Money can't buy me love.' I loved London. I felt like I had been born to live there. I loved the buzz, the Tube, the lights, the people, in fact, everything!

Every pay day was like Christmas. We would rush headlong down Kensington Church Street to *Biba*, the hottest boutique in town. A young designer called Mary Quant was just beginning to make a name for herself there. Our wages were just eight pounds per week, but with no rent and food bills, what else was there for us to do but spend it on the latest fashions. After all, we had figures like Twiggy. We had long legs, and miniskirts had just hit the scene in a big way. We were in heaven. With one pay packet, I bought a black shiny mini wet-look coat, white shiny wet-look knee-high boots with three-inch platform heels and a tiny red tartan miniskirt with matching perky jockey cap. What a doll. Uggh. And I still had enough left over for a night out on the town.

Pubs still abided by the daily holy hours in the sixties, so each day between 2 and 5 pm, we were free. These hours for me were spent getting the Tube to Charing Cross, buying a bag of fresh cherries from the fruit sellers, and sitting on the canvas deckchairs listening to the military bands that played there every afternoon. Pure bliss. The sound of the trombones and clarinets, the warmth of the sunshine and the smell of the grass transported me to another world. A world unknown to me in Galway.

All summer, I had saved my many tips in an empty Drambuie bottle on the shelf of the bar, and all too soon it was time to empty it out and buy my return ticket to Dublin. My boyfriend was inconsolable. Devastated. How would he survive without me? He begged me to stay as all holiday romantics do. But thankfully, I kept my reasoning intact. The vision of my father's face if I did not get back home quickly was deterrent enough to accepting the marriage proposals that reigned down on my head daily. When I left him at Heathrow at the end of September, they needed buckets and mops to dry the tears from the departure area.

But I promised myself that I would be back in London for good. Yes, once I finished university. Promises, Promises.

2

London 1998

*T*hirty years later. May 26th to be exact. We were on a horrific journey that had already taken nine hours. And heading south for London on the M1, with the rain and the mist everywhere, I started to cry, thinking I wouldn't be able to keep going. But the little soldier, my son Luke, saved the day by talking me through it all. Never once did he complain. He just sat beside me and kept me entertained. It was as though he totally understood what I was going through. He recounted tales from school, sang all his favourite songs, and explained in great detail the entire plot of the film he had seen in the cinema the previous week. On and on he went. I was so blessed to have him.

Earlier that day, a rotten grey cold mist covered Dun Laoghaire harbour. We sat in the queue of cars, waiting for the 8 am ferry to Holyhead to begin loading. My mind was numb, my body cold and tight. I sat there staring out through the mist, and I could feel the pressure of the tears building up behind my eyes. But it was too early in the day to start crying in front of my little comrade. I got out of the car, using the excuse that I was going to enquire about sailing times. As I walked between the rows of waiting vehicles, I struggled to keep my composure. Each time I saw a couple in a car, I got worse. When I saw families with children, I felt worse again. They all looked so happy. I pictured the children's excitement at the prospect of going on holiday. Maybe they were going camping on the west coast of France, as we had done as a family 15 years previously.

I looked back up towards Dun Laoghaire town, and wondered where my husband was now. I had learnt from the newspaper six weeks earlier that he was renting a flat somewhere in Dun Laoghaire. The exact location was still a secret he kept from me. I imagined that he was up there now, looking out over the bay from his window, laughing at my plight. Those thoughts did me no good whatsoever, but were impossible to erase from my mind. Whenever I opened my eyes, I could see him. His face was indelibly printed on my mind's eye forever.

Twenty-four hours earlier, I had packed my life into the back of my old Mazda car, and driven away from my home in Donegal. I had strapped my young son into the passenger seat and fled, without telling friend or foe. As I left the driveway I dared not look back. I did not want to see the shrubs I had planted, the garden I had tended, and the trees I had pruned. The tears were burning inside my eyes but I dared not let even one of them escape, lest he would see.

"I will try it for two weeks, Mum, but if we don't like it, will you promise me we can come back?" Luke had said before getting into the car.

"I promise."

But I did not believe my own words. He was nine-years-old and I was taking him away from the only world he knew.

During the previous two weeks, I had talked to him about the prospect of both of us going to live in London. He was not happy with the idea. Nor was I. I had no wish to leave behind my home, my job, my friends and everything else I had built up over my twenty-five years in Donegal. But eventually the situation had deteriorated to such an extent that I knew I would not see my next birthday, if I did not make my escape as quickly as possible. My daughter, who lived in London with her husband and baby, had rung me that day at lunchtime and pleaded with me.

"Mum, please get out of there," she repeated. "Please come to London and let me look after you. We'll do up a good CV for you, and

help you find a job and a nice flat. Please don't stay there any longer."
I knew she was right.

I rang my eldest son in Dublin and he too was relieved.

"Just look out for the numbers on the motorway, Mum," he advised.
"Don't look for the names of towns or cities and you'll be fine. Just ring
me when you get there."

When my little boy came home from school that Monday afternoon,
I had the car almost ready to go. At 6 pm, I locked my front door behind
me and drove away. It was as instant as that. I vowed never to return.

Once we were out on the Irish Sea, we felt a bit better. Kids love big
ships and mine was no exception. It had all his favourite video games
and McDonald's, so he was in heaven. I wished that we could just stay
out there forever, going round and round in big circles. Then we would
never have to face whatever fate awaited us on the other side. But three
short hours later we were in Holyhead, and I was forced to drive onto
foreign soil. My body was trembling. As we set off through the bleak
Welsh countryside, I felt terrified. It must have been this overpowering
terror, which caused me to forget my older son's good advice, and after
two hours, we were hopelessly lost. We should have emerged onto the
motorway towards London within a couple of hours, but instead ended
up driving in ever-increasing circles around Wales for over four hours.
Normally my sense of direction had been excellent, but now all of my
senses were disorientated and panic and mental exhaustion had set in.

By 5 pm having at last found the motorway, we were still hours from
London and I began to cry again from tiredness and despair. The rain
and mist and greyness never let up since we had driven off the boat in
Holyhead. It was as though it were saying to me, 'I told you not to do
this. Why did you not listen?'

"It's okay, Mum," said a little voice beside me.

"We'll be okay. Let's see if we can find a place to stop on the
motorway and get something to eat."

Such a logical head on such young shoulders. One hour later, after some 'plastic' motorway refreshments and a stretch of our legs, we were on our way feeling more relaxed and more hopeful. At 10 pm that night, we pulled up outside my daughter's home in Croydon. Her husband had guided us for the last few miles by mobile phone, like an air traffic controller at Heathrow, guiding us in to land through the mist. They were relieved to see us and for the first time in weeks, I felt safe. I thanked God for having given birth to that wonderful girl.

The following morning it was time to set my plan into action. But I felt so physically and mentally drained. The last few weeks in Ireland had been a horrifying nightmare and events had taken their toll on my general well being. I had not eaten or slept adequately for six weeks, and I had been relying on pills of all sorts to get me through the days. I had lost almost two stone, and my skin was beginning to sag. Things could only get better I hoped. But there was no time to be lost. I had to get my son settled into a school as quickly as possible. I had a cheque for £5,000 in my purse, but knew it would not last for long. This was what I had always called my 'Rainy Day Fund'. I had gathered every penny I could find for over twenty years and stashed it away secretly for this day. The day when something would hurt me so much that I would be forced to get out. Now, it was all I had to put a deposit on a flat, pay school fees, and to keep us going until I found a job. But first of all, I had to find us somewhere to live.

3

A Place to Call Home

"Hello, Brent's Estate Agents. Can I help you?"

"Yes, I see you have a property to rent in Warham Road. Can you tell me if it is still available?"

The previous twenty places I rang had *just* been taken.

"Yes Madam, it is still available."

My spirits soared. Success at last. Two bedrooms, one living room/kitchen and one bathroom. Rent £700 per month. On the third floor. No lift, but what the heck. It would be *Home!* Perfect. At last we would be able to move out of my daughter's house, where we had shared a bedroom with the baby. My son had slept on the floor beside the baby's cot, while I had the luxury of the bed. However, now came the really difficult part.

"Are you employed?" he asked.

"No, not at present," I replied innocently.

"Sorry. No DHSS. Goodbye."

He was gone. He hung up, just like that. I almost cried. In my ignorance then, I did not even know what the DHSS was. Was it some type of animal? Was it some sort of foreign asylum seeker? I was later to find out all about it, much to my chagrin. I suppose the estate agent did have a point. I had no job. I had no income. So how was I going to pay rent on a flat? I felt like a criminal.

At least my son's schooling had been sorted out while I had tried to find us a place to live. Fortunately, a friend, whose children had attended one junior school, had recommended me to the Principal. Luckily, he agreed to accept my son the week after I arrived. There were only one hundred pupils, both boys and girls. At least at that size, he stood a better chance of settling in quickly rather than being plunged into a crowded school. I paid the fees for his first term there, and would just have to find the next set of fees somehow. But after one day in school, he loved it. His face told it all when I went to pick him up that first afternoon.

"It's brilliant, Mum," he gushed with excitement. "One of the boy's grandparents are from Donegal. We even played football at lunchtime and I scored two goals!"

Well, thank God for that at least. He looked so cute and gorgeous in his lovely uniform with blue blazer, grey shorts and striped knee socks. I stood him outside in the street and took loads of photographs. I felt so proud of him. It had cost me a lot to kit him out with uniform, shoes, boots, rugby kit, cricket whites, special school-bag, special kit bag, etc. but it was worth it all to see him smiling. No matter what it cost, if I had to scrub floors to earn money, I had to put his security and happiness first. He deserved that from me. He had been put through enough upset already in his short life.

I had also started looking for a job the day after I arrived, but these things took time, and I had to wait a week just to get an interview with a temping agency. In the meantime, I was in limbo. I tried another estate agent. I decided to forget about honesty and lie a little, if this was what was required. This time when the agent said a flat was still available, I was ready for him.

"Are you working at present?" he asked.

"I will be paying with private income," I assured him very quickly.

I had the £5,000 less the school costs and would have to use this money to get us set up.

"Do you have proof of this income?" he asked.

"What sort of proof?" I enquired.

"Can you supply us with your bank account details for the past six months."

I was stuck. I did not have an account with a British bank. So, no bank account, no job, equals no flat. Next morning, I set off to the bank planning to open an account and lodge my sterling draft. No problem there, I anticipated. The young man behind the counter in the bank was very pleasant and welcoming.

"Good morning, Madam. Can I help you?" he said.

"Yes, thank you. I would like to open a bank account please," I announced, smiling back at him. He looked at me as though seeing a prehistoric monster.

"I'm sorry, Madam, but you will have to make an appointment to see the manager," he replied haughtily.

It must have been a long time since I had opened a bank account because I never remembered it being so difficult. Or was that just in Ireland? In Britain, I was being looked upon with all the suspicion of a criminal. Perhaps it was my Irish accent. Was he just waiting for me to draw a loaded gun from my handbag? I made a quick mental note to disguise my accent in future when dealing with people in authority.

"Okay, how long will he be?" I asked, thinking he would say maybe five minutes or one hour.

"I'm afraid it will be at least a week before he can see you. He is extremely busy," he replied.

He could not supply this appointment for over a week, and further informed me that it would then take at least ten working days, or two weeks in layman's language, for the account to become accessible. In the meantime, I would have to provide written proof of a full twenty-five-year history of my life and financial position. I would possibly need proof of everything I had eaten for breakfast for the past ten years! I would need guarantees from the butcher, the baker and the candlestick maker! I had a banker's draft for £5,000 sterling in my pocket but no one would take it from me. It was now as much use as a train ticket to trackless Donegal!

Even when I got access to it, how long would it last us anyway, I wondered. If I was lucky, I was about to sign a lease on a flat for six months, at possibly £700 per month. That left £4,300. Minus a £700 deposit. That left £3,600. I had borrowed £1,000 from my daughter for school fees and all that, so it left £2,600. I would also have to pay £100 per month council tax, and water rates on top of that. I worked it out that if I could not get a decent job, then we could not survive any longer than two months at the most, and that would be pushing it. All I wanted was a place to live. A place where I could unpack our belongings. But it was like trying to move forward harnessed to a bulldozer travelling in the opposite direction. I felt like giving up. But I went on and eventually, two weeks later, I had a bank account.

Then it was back to finding an available flat. Finally, I got one. I went to look at it and it was prefect. Well, as perfect as we were going to get. A caravan would have done me at that stage. The owner was going abroad for a year and the flat was empty. Just ready and waiting for us to unpack the car boot and take up residence.

"Yes, we should be able to complete the agreement within three weeks," the agent informed me.

Three weeks? My God, now what were they talking about?

"Can I not just move in this weekend?" I pleaded.

Again that strange look of incredulity from the letting agent. Was I crazy? This was London after all. No, things had to be done properly and this would take time. After all, the agency had to be seen to be doing something to earn their enormous fees. Contracts had to be drawn up. Inventories had to be taken. Suitable references had to be obtained.

So who could I get to provide a reference saying that I would look after this property carefully? I had not lived in rented accommodation since I was a student. Should I perhaps ask my husband to provide a reference, I wondered. After all, he was the only person I had lived with since I had left my parent's home as a young bride. Would he write: *I guarantee that this woman has kept my house in a suitable condition for twenty-eight years. I guarantee that she will not smash up the furniture, throw wild drug parties, or terrorise the neighbours.* Perhaps he wouldn't give me a favourable reference. How was I to know? I wasn't sure of anything any more. Luckily, I was able to speak directly to the owner, and she was satisfied with that.

Eventually, everything was sorted and moving day dawned. I was met in the hallway by the owner's mother, who would go through the inventory with me, step-by-step, page-by-boring-page. Yes, three plastic egg cups, one cracked. Yes, brown carpet in bedroom, slightly stained under window. Yes, plastic potted plant in bathroom, missing three petals from the flower in the centre. Yes, six knives, five forks, four spoons and three tea-stained mugs. On and on it went. The endless graphic detail I endured. I felt like giving her back her egg cups and her plant and the rest of the cheap grimy contents and telling her where to put them. But, I resisted. Once she had gone, I packed her baubles into the nearest empty closet, never to be seen again by me, at least. I then retrieved my prized possessions from the boot of my car, where they had been since my departure from Ireland weeks earlier.

It was a strange assortment of belongings that I had grabbed from my home in the hours before my flight, but all with a purpose, nonetheless. My computer, because I wanted to keep on writing. My stereo, so that even in the midst of darkness I could play my favourite classical music. My photographs showing my children in the good times. My wonderful memories. My violin. Maybe I would get the time and the peace of mind to play it again. My books and my paints, just in case I got the time for either. And, of course, my microwave oven. In fact, all the threads of my past life for me to cling to.

4

Not Jim or Jimmy, but James

"Who's that guy who's always saying hello to everyone?" I asked my friend Ann one day. We were hanging about the Archway in UCG one day in October 1968 trying to settle in after our wonderful summer in London.

"Isn't he that guy from Donegal, who was in our Pre-Med class last year? He's supposed to be very friendly. Apparently these Donegal fellows seem to say hello to everyone," Ann replied.

A concept unknown to us Galwegians. It was my first recollected sighting of my husband. Admittedly, I had never really noticed him in the previous year, even though we had attended all the same lectures.

When my schoolmates and I joined the hallowed ranks of UCG in 1967, it was in the glorious days of being allowed to study for whatever degree one fancied. The only passport for entry was the 'One Honour' in the Leaving Cert. I had got my honour, and so I was in. On that Tuesday morning when 'College' opened, six of us met at the front gate. None of us had quite decided what course we were going to try, even though we had discussed it all at length the day before. Sadly, not a lot of career guidance in those days. None, in fact.

As it turned out, there was a three-way split, with two of us for Science, two for Arts, and two for Medicine, myself being of the latter persuasion. Once signed on, we all met at Ma Craven's Coffee Shop in the university grounds at lunchtime to swap details. I studied Medicine for a year, but I found all the physics and chemistry very boring. I enjoyed biology however. But I decided halfway through the year that it was not for me.

However, it was a wonderful year socially, as I was going out with a very nice medical student two years older than me called Tom. Amazingly, the only huge difference between him and all the other fellows was that he did not drink. I never really had a problem with that, but because the entire crowd we hung around with were all drinkers, I felt that perhaps he was not really enjoying himself.

"Why don't you get him to try a drink?" my friends would urge.

"Why? He doesn't want to, so I can't force him," I replied defensively.

I think it bothered them more than it bothered me. He did however play the guitar and he was a great singer, so this was a much bigger attraction for me. I had been studying the piano since I was five, and the guitar in later years, and simply loved anything to do with music. Some of our dates were spent with him teaching me new chords and new songs.

One Sunday night in February 1968, there was a folk concert in 'The Aula', the main entertainment hub of the college. My boyfriend and two of his roommates had asked me to join them singing some Bob Dylan numbers on stage. I was thrilled, as I had always wanted to sing with a folk group. Halfway through the concert, we were sitting by the stage just preparing to go on, when suddenly, the main doors of the Aula burst open. As the audience turned around to see what was going on, the UCG Soccer Team made a triumphant and noisy entrance and proceeded to make their way onto the stage, followed by a large band of cheering supporters. Apparently, they had just arrived back from Cork, where the previous day they had won the coveted Collingwood Cup for Intervarsity Soccer. The most important sports trophy in the College calendar, as I was to discover in the following years. However, at that time I had no interest whatsoever in soccer, and we were disgusted that our stage debut had been foiled. The excitement was tremendous, as they hoisted the Cup above the crowd, and sang and shouted for the rest of the night. Needless to say the concert was abandoned, and we never got to sing that Bob Dylan number. As all the players were introduced one by one, I vaguely remember the captain saying that the youngest player on the victorious team was a good-looking Pre-Med student from Donegal. But I didn't actually catch his name.

That summer, as I mentioned, I had gone to work in London, but broke up with the guitar player before I left. I knew London would be too much of a temptation to go out with other boys. And I wasn't the two-timing type. After I returned to UCG in October, I opted for the Arts Faculty. I had definitely decided that Medicine and I would not work. Instead I would study languages.

Every Tuesday night the students union held a dance in Seapoint, the dancing Mecca of the West. The usual crowd of us went along every week. However, on one particular night in November, none of us were in the mood for going out. I had settled down at home, when my friend Cathy rang.

"Please come tonight, Marguerite. Peter's friend told me they're all going, and I just have to go and 'lift' him," she begged.

"Well, okay then, but I'm leaving the minute you get him," I warned.

I couldn't let her go on her own, and she was desperate to get off with this guy. With no time to wash my hair, I donned my long brown hairpiece. Wow! They had been all the rage in London that summer. My own hair was shortish at the time, so this gave me a totally different appearance.

To pass the time while my friend went hunting, I took a stroll upstairs to the balcony to see if there was anyone interesting about. The balcony circled above three sides of the dance floor, so it was a good place to go and see what was on offer below. As I was passing some fellows, I heard someone saying hello. It was the smiley guy from Donegal. I walked on but glanced back casually to see if he was still there. He caught my eye but I looked away shyly. I looked back again a few seconds later, and he was still looking at me, so I kept eye contact, as it was always a good way of seeing if someone was interested. Then he vanished, and I went back downstairs to the dance floor. There was no bar to hang out of in those days, just a shop selling minerals. One minute later, 'he' appeared from nowhere, right in front of me.

"Will you dance?" he asked.

Well, it was the sixties and things were more formal. I was not at all in the mood for 'lifting' anyone that night, and certainly not a total stranger. Well, anyone from outside Galway City was considered a stranger. I was annoyed with myself for perhaps having encouraged him by looking back at him, and now had no choice but to dance with him. And so I did. He was wearing a hand-knitted brown Aran jumper and brown trousers. (Even to this day I'm not fond of brown clothes on him.) He told me that he played soccer, and had won the Collingwood Cup with UCG.

"You put a very sudden end to my singing career," I joked.

He laughed.

That night he told me that he never took a drink and I thought, here we go again. I had broken up with one boyfriend who did not drink and now here was another teetotaller. Quite ironic that, as later years would show.

Near the end of the night, he came back for a second round of the floor, and then asked if he could walk me home. I said okay as my friend had succeeded in capturing her prey and had plans of her own. I arranged to meet him outside. To my horror, he was wearing a huge stiff shiny black anorak. A young aspiring Bertie, perhaps. I suppose he was hoping to grow into it. When we got to my house, he put his arms and the big anorak around me, and kissed me. I was totally unimpressed, I must say. Maybe the anorak was getting in the way, or suffocating me with the smell of rubber. A real passion killer. He said goodnight, so obviously he had got the message. Anyway, he was going home to Donegal the following day for the mid-term break. I was not too worried really as I had my eye on someone else and I was taking my time.

The following Tuesday night, we were all back after the break, and I went to Seapoint with all my friends. We had all regained our cheerfulness and energy and zest for dancing and 'lifting', and were ready for a good night's fun. I had barely walked in the door of the dancehall, when who should appear but the Donegal boy. James McDaid he had told me his name was. Not Jim or Jimmy, but James. Nice name, I had thought at the time.

That night, I could not believe my eyes. What a transformation! He looked good enough to eat. He was wearing the most beautiful navy corduroy suit, a blue shirt and a navy tie, and gorgeous tan leather moccasins. He told me his aunt had bought them for him in America that summer, while he was working there. He was grinning from ear to ear, and full of life, not at all the reserved boy that I had met the previous week. He asked me out to dance, and we got on great together. He told me that he had dressed up especially to impress me. And he succeeded.

That night I was wearing my pride and joy of the London fashion scene. A tiny bottle green suit, with a minisculish short skirt, and a very tightly fitted waisted jacket, zipped up to my chin. I was also wearing white shiny knee-high boots, a fashion statement unheard of in Ireland at the time. And I had got rid of my wig, which impressed him no end. We looked fabulous together. Just like Twiggy and George Best. We danced all night after that, and never looked at anyone else. I was amazed when I learned that he had gone for two pints with his friends, before he came to the dance! He was no longer booze-free.

"Do you want to come out with me on Thursday night?" he asked.

"Okay," I replied.

On Thursday night, we met outside the Coachman Hotel in Dominick Street. When we went inside to buy drinks, I saw him pull a five-pound note from his pocket. I was shocked. How many people apart from my father on pay day owned a five-pound note? It must have been his entire month's allowance, but it didn't seem to bother him to spend it on drink.

"Oh, I won that on the horses," he said when he sat down.

Not even a tinkle of a warning bell rang in my head. I had a wonderful time with him, and couldn't wait for him to ask me out again.

The wait was very short. The following morning after my first lecture, he came and asked me to go out with him on Saturday night. I knew then that he fancied me, and I was beginning to fancy him a bit too. After that weekend, there was no keeping us apart. We spent every available second together. We studied together. We ate together. We drank together. As he was no longer a non-drinker, every date was spent in the pub, mainly the Skeff, in Eyre Square. There was always plenty of fun around him, socialising with the soccer team, whether in victory or defeat. In fact, there was always a reason for celebration, be it good or bad. He was also very warm and open and affectionate with me and we would talk for hours, but never felt we had enough time to say all the things we wanted to say. When he went home to Donegal for Christmas, we wrote to each other every day. He didn't have a phone nearby, so some days he walked to the nearest village to use the public phone there. My father would tease me good-naturedly about him.

"I see on the news that Donegal is covered in snow and I spotted that young fellow of yours up there minding sheep on the mountains."

"Ha! Ha! Ha! Very funny!"

However, they were to build a wonderful friendship over the following four years; the aspiring young doctor giving the father-in-law invaluable comfort on his premature deathbed.

At that time, where Galway people were concerned, Donegal was as far away as China. An undiscovered world. Anywhere north of Knock was 'injun territory'. But James came back early after Christmas, before college reopened, as he missed me so much. He told his mother he was coming back early to study. He never opened a book.

For months afterwards he pursued me relentlessly. It was as though he gave up on everything else in his life to be with me. He sat beside me every day in the study hall, waited for me outside lecture theatres, ate with me, came to my house every night, and, in general, never left my side. He was besotted. Or, as I look back now, he was addicted to me, in the same way he become addicted to many things in life, including politics.

The following summer, I was due to spend three months in France as an *au pair*. The Côte d'Azur to be exact. I was really looking forward to it, but at the last moment James talked me into going to America with him instead. We would get jobs in New York, he promised. I could always go to the South of France some other time, he convinced me. A big mistake, I later realised, but then, love is blind. At the time, he convinced me that he could not bear to be apart from me for three months, so I bought my ticket for New York, much to the annoyance of my parents. But they knew I was strong-willed, and gave in eventually. After all, I was now nineteen and naturally, I knew everything!

One year later, we were married. We were the happiest pair in town. In the early seventies, it was not unusual to marry young. All around us, students were tying the knot and producing babies, in that order. It was still hippie and flower power time. The future was a glorious colourful canvas. There was only two years to go before he would be qualified as a doctor. He could not wait to get money, so that we wouldn't have to rely on our parents to help us out. And typical of the way things were done in the early seventies, we had three children in the space of five years. The theory our friends bandied around was to have them all within a short space of time and let them grow up together. And so we did. Well, they didn't cost anything, did they? They came free, or so we were led to believe. I wonder how many of our generation would turn the clocks back now if they could, and copy the British tradition of leaving four years between each child. When I tell my daughter now of having three children in nappies and bottles at the same time, she cringes. But we still had time to enjoy ourselves and have a good social life. There was no such thing as holidays or fancy houses with fancy furniture, but we were deliriously happy. We loved each other and that was all that mattered. An easier life was always just around the corner.

5

Medical Secretary for Hire

I stood on the corner of Bond Street, and trembled with fear and desperation. I had to do it. I had to keep my nerve. I had to do it for my son especially. I just had to find us a job in London.

During my first week in London, I had rang around all the local employment agencies looking for work. I had been told that there was plenty of secretarial work available and that I could expect to have an interview in approximately two weeks. But why then did everything have to take so long in this part of the world? That would mean it could be a month before I might get a job. That was no good to me.

Apart from the money aspect, I desperately needed to be busy. I had to work in order to distract my mind from the mess my life was in. I decided the local agencies in Croydon were likely to be of little use and I was better off checking out Central London where work would surely be readily available. In the meantime, I contacted all the large supermarkets in the area; Tesco's, Sainsbury's, Waitrose. Well, at least I could stack shelves or push buttons on a till if required. I was willing to do anything to earn a few bob. I even replied to an advert for a cook and housekeeper in a large country residence in Surrey. There was no limit to what I would do. Anything to prevent me from having to crawl back to Donegal.

I contacted the agency in Bond Street who had advertised for medical secretaries and they agreed to see me the following Monday morning.

So there I stood on Bond Street, ten minutes before my interview wondering if I could hold on to my nerve. In my jacket pocket, I took out my little bottle labelled 'Rescue Remedy'. A friend had given it to me three weeks earlier when I was in dire need. Now that need for courage and guidance was with me again and as I placed two drops on the back of my tongue, I also asked God to help me.

The agency offices were plush and spacious. With a smile of confidence on my face that I did not feel, I made myself known to the receptionist and was instructed to take a seat. I looked over at the other 'contestants' seated along the wall and my heart sank. None of them looked older than twenty-five. Here I was, within spitting distance of half a century, and I was competing against these toddlers. I felt like a total greenhorn compared to these perky young things. But I held my head up high and smiled. I knew that I looked the part. Thankfully, in my haste to leave Donegal, I had snatched a smart navy suit from my wardrobe, and I was glad of it now. Teamed with a crisp white shirt from M&S, I could have fooled the chairman of ICI. Now all I had to do was convince them that I could perform.

I was ushered into an interview room where a young man, no older than my own adult son, proceeded to question me. I wanted to make a run for it.

"Okay, Marguerite, we'll start off with some tests. All in all, these should only take about two hours, next some typing speed tests, some medical vocabulary tests and then we'll test your computer skills."

"Okay," I swallowed hard.

"After that we will interview you, and then take it from there," he finished.

I could feel the sweat breaking out on the palms of my hands. My God, my mind was in no way ready for any type of test, I thought. I felt my knees go weak and my head began to spin. It had been over six weeks since I had left my job at the local hospital in Letterkenny one Friday evening, with the intention of being back there again on Monday morning. But so much had happened in the meantime and I had not been anywhere near a computer since. Could I even remember how to create a file? I was not sure. As promised, my daughter had typed me up a 'nice tight' CV, but could I live up to it? I wasn't sure.

You have to try, you have to try, a voice kept screeching in my head. I thought of my son. By some unfathomable miracle I managed the typing test with few errors and reasonable speed even though my fingers had turned to jelly. I began to relax.

Then the vocabulary test. I had always been the best in the class at spelling. Ever since I was four-years-old. I loved spelling. The harder and longer the word, the better.

Which of the following five spellings is the correct one?

Haemorage. Hemorage. Haemorrhage. Hemorheag. Haemorrage.

The words swam before me like fish in a tank. Focus. Focus, my mind told me. It was a word I had spelt a million times in the past ten years in my job, but my mind was in turmoil. And there were twenty more multiple-choice bear traps to navigate my way through.

Create a database using the following information.

Oh, dear God. I had not used databases since I did an IT course twelve years earlier. But I managed it. By some hand of God, I managed it. I was over the first hurdle.

Next, the interview. During it I relied on my imagination to colourfully embellish my previous experience. I just had to hope they wouldn't go to the bother of checking up on it. Luckily, I eventually managed to convince them that I could be relied upon to hold down one of the jobs they had on offer.

"Well, you are in luck," said the nice young man.

"I think that we might have just the position to suit you, and they are extremely anxious to get someone to start as soon as possible."

My heart leapt at his words.

"Would you like me to set up an interview with them for this afternoon? Say four o'clock?"

I was exhausted and drained after leaving home at 10 am that morning. I had no time for lunch, as my interview had run from 11.30 am to 2 pm. But I was desperate.

"Yes, that would be great," I replied with as much enthusiasm as I could muster.

"Right, if you leave now, you should just make it in time," he replied.

More travelling. More Tubes. I popped into the Ladies before I left and surveyed the ghost in the mirror. I just wanted to go home, pull the bedcovers over my head and never get up again. I wanted the whole nightmare to be over. But with a dash of make-up, a redo of the lipstick and a squirt of perfume, I was back on the trail. My destination was a private GP practice in the City, the financial centre of London. I had absolutely no experience of working in a GP practice, but had told them at the interview hours earlier that I had been running my husband's practice for the past twenty years. If they only knew how he would barely even let me in the door of it, no matter how often I had begged him for a job.

"You can't get on with people," he had accused.

But I was going to bluff my way through the interview, if it killed me. If I had to lie, then I would lie. Our future depended on it.

The practice manager loved me. I was just what they were looking for, she said. Their clientele were drawn from the big financial and legal institutions in the City – all the top British solicitors, bankers, corporate managers, etc. She needed a mature and competent person with experience to deal with clients on reception. Well, that should be no bother to me. I had been dealing with men in high places on the political circuit and knew what they wanted. I would not let myself be fazed by them, or intimidated if they became over-demanding or abusive in any way. In fact, few of the patients were actually ill. The eight GPs generally dealt with insurance medicals, vaccinations for employees being sent overseas, work fitness assessments, and so on. The doctor who actually owned the practice also interviewed me and assured me that I would be perfect for the job.

By the end of the day they promised that following further discussion among themselves, they would phone me the next day and let me know if they would offer me the job. I left the practice floating on a cloud. It was 5 pm and all around me workers were pouring out of hundreds of offices and heading for their trains. Would this be me the following week? Would I be part of this heaving exciting workforce? At last there was a bright light beckoning. I spotted a pub around the corner and made a run for it.

Five minutes later with a large glass of red wine in front of me, I relived the events of that day. It had been tough but I had survived. I had lied, I had bluffed and I had exaggerated beyond my wildest notions. But, hopefully, I was in. I was sure of it. My son was elated when I got home and told him my news. We danced around the room hugging each other and shouting. Poor kid. I hadn't been quite as aware as perhaps I should have been, how worrying our financial situation had been for him. Indeed, he was to grow up pretty quickly in the next few months.

First thing next morning the phone rang. It was the practice manager. The job was mine. They would like me to start the following Monday. We were now settled in our flat and all was rosy. But since I would not be getting home from London until 7 pm each evening and my son finished school at 3 pm, I had to sort out a childminder. I would be dropping him to school at 7.45 am before getting my train to London, so it was going to be a really long day for him. But he assured me that he would be okay. He had been put into a strange school, in a strange country, with strange classmates and strange teachers, and now he was going to be looked after by a stranger after school for four hours. But once again, he never complained. I felt a totally overwhelming love for him all through those difficult times. Even if he had been part of a family with brothers and sisters his own age to share his thoughts with, then moving to a strange country would have been difficult enough. But he did not even have such family security behind him. Luckily, I did find a very nice Irish lady, recommended to me by the Principal, and she quickly made him feel at home.

Work was wonderful. I absolutely loved it. All the staff were very friendly apart from one lady, who was effectively the office 'Head Girl'. But I made a vow not to let her get to me and smiled sweetly at her whenever she spoke or passed me on the stairs. I was not going to allow anything or anyone to spoil my happiness. At the interview the previous week, they had discussed a temporary contract, possibly from month to month. However, by my second day in the job, they were so satisfied with me that they asked me to sign a permanent contract straightaway. They were delighted with the way I handled the clients, both on the telephone and in person, and my computer skills were far beyond what they had expected.

"In fact, I can see you taking over my job in a few months, as I want to go back to part-time working," said the practice manager.

I had even agreed to sign a permanent contract on the following Monday for £17,000 per annum with the possibility of promotion. At the time, I could hardly believe what I was hearing.

The work was well within my capabilities and I could see no problems on the road ahead. I got on well with everyone and they all complimented me on how quickly I had settled in to my new post. Life was good. My son was happy in school and the flat was comfortable enough. Maybe now we could relax for a few months and get our heads sorted. Maybe.

Beware the light at the end of the tunnel. It may be an oncoming train. How often had I experienced that during the previous twenty-five years? It was Friday afternoon at 3.30 pm, when the phone on my desk rang.

"Marguerite, this is Dave from the agency. I'm sorry, I have some bad news. They won't be needing you next week after all. I'm really sorry. I don't know what has happened."

"Do you mean they want me back the week after that?" I asked quizzically.

"No. They don't want you to come back at all," he replied in an embarrassed voice.

I was dumbstruck. He explained that he had received a call from the owner of the practice stating that they did not need me after all. That was it. She had offered him no explanation when asked for one. He could not understand it, as only the previous day they had been pressing the agency to let me sign a permanent contract. Agencies prefer to keep you temping, as they get a commission from the employer. But they had even agreed to let me sign the permanent contract. There was nothing Dave could do. And to make matters worse he could not get me any work for the following week as all temping jobs had been filled earlier in the week. The practice manager had already left for the day, and the owner also.

I got up from my desk and walked out of the building. My head was reeling. My stomach was sick. I walked into the pub where only a week earlier I had rejoiced. I ordered a brandy and felt I was going to die. I couldn't drink it. My throat seemed to have sealed up and I was gasping for oxygen. I got up again and walked back into the street. I don't know how many hours I walked around. I was in total shock. Somewhere in London, I went down into a Tube station and started to make the long journey home to Surrey.

Back at the flat, I fought to keep an air of jollity in front of my son. Once he fell asleep that night, I dropped into a black despair. I went over and over again in my head every word and every action since the previous day. Was it something that I had said or done that had caused them to change their minds so drastically? All weekend I bluffed to my daughter and son-in-law, pretending that I was so happy. But my husband had been right all along. I was useless. I was a failure. He had told me that I could not get anything right. He told me that I would come running back home with my tail tucked between my legs. Now I had proved him right.

On Monday morning I got up and got dressed for work as usual. I took my son to school telling him that I was rushing for my train. Then I drove back to the flat and wept. I wept till my head and body were empty of tears. I did not know where to turn. I was right back at square one, except now I was living a lie as well. I could not bear to heap any more worry onto my daughter's shoulders. She had her own life and did not need to be dragged down with me. I spent the entire day ringing employment agencies all over London. None could give me an interview until the end of the week.

The agency I was registered with promised they would get in touch if they had anything, but didn't think it was likely. They did tell me in confidence, however, that they had experienced some problems with that particular GP practice in the past. They had let some other employees go in the same manner as I had been, without any explanation forthcoming. I phoned one of the ladies who had befriended me during my brief employ, and she filled me in on the office gossip. Apparently, the 'Head Girl' had been giving unsavoury reports about me to the boss, behind everyone's back. It transpired that this particular individual had a major problem with other races, especially Irish, invading her workplace.

So that was it. Felled at the stump for being Irish. Had I been as aware then as I am now of racial discrimination in the workplace, I would have fought back. But I was a struggling mother on my own, and in no fit state to stand up for myself. However, all of that would change as I gained strength and courage over the coming months and years.

All week I scoured the newspapers in the hope of something. I wrote dozens of job application letters, but knew it would be ages before I would get a response. What was I going to do in the short term? I had no options. I was just a failure and my husband had got it right again. This thought went round and round in my mind day and night, never giving up. Failure. Failure. Failure.

My daughter eventually discovered that I had not gone to work on Monday or Tuesday and was annoyed with me.

"I'm not feeling well," I lied.

"You're not going to make a very good impression, if you start taking days off just after you've started," she retorted.

I knew where she was coming from. In her eyes, I had landed the job of my dreams and there I was putting it in danger straightaway. But I still couldn't tell her. Eventually, by Wednesday, I had to come clean. I asked her to meet me in the car outside her house, and I told her. I was crying and very upset. She did her best to console me, but I was very down. Because I had no answering machine in the flat, I had to stay by the phone all day in case the agencies would ring back. By Friday there was still nothing, even for the following week. Even the supermarkets were not taking on staff.

Then on Saturday morning, I got a letter from the original agency telling me there was a few days work at King's College Hospital in London. They asked for me to report there the following Monday morning to the research department. I was familiar with this hospital situated in Dulwich, as coincidentally it was where my daughter had studied for her degree. At least it would be something for a few days, I thought. My spirits picked up again. Unfortunately, however, the trains did not run from my area to Dulwich directly so I headed off on the bus on Monday morning at 7.30 am. One and a half hours later, I climbed out of a stuffy, noisy horrible bus and was both mentally and physically exhausted. My head was splitting.

I found my way to the office where I was to work. It was a really old hospital located in a terribly rundown area and full of colourful nationalities. I was put to work for an Iranian professor. He was a chain-smoker and believed that women were an inferior species. Not surprisingly, his previous secretary had walked out the previous Friday. So there was no one on hand to tell me what the job entailed or to give me any direction. I slogged away on the phone and computer all day. Every so often, cheroot-face would come in, roar some instructions at me and disappear again.

At last it was lunchtime, and I looked for somewhere to eat. I followed the signposts for the cafeteria and joined the queue for the mass-produced vittels. I sat at a table among a crowd of strangers, moving the soggy mass around my plate. I felt so alone. What was I doing here, in this awful place, where no one even spoke to me? That evening, as I climbed out of the bus at 7.30 pm, I was desperate. The thought of having to repeat the entire charade again the following day had me in tears once more.

Next morning, I packed myself an appetising sandwich, saving me from a trip to the canteen again. And even if it meant taking ten different trains, I decided not to undergo that bus journey again. At lunchtime, I headed out into the sunshine, hoping to find a park where I could sit and eat my lunch. Sadly, the only place available was the hospital car park. There were no coffee bars or cafés around. Just blocks of high-rise flats. As I went back inside, a huge African guy of about eighty, in gaudy clothes, tried to chat me up.

"Hey, you got time for me baby?" he whispered conspiratorially.

I felt sick and terrified. At this point, I felt so alone and scared believing that I could not go on for very long more.

Towards the end of the second day, however, the agency rang. I had to finish up that day, as the professor was going away unexpectedly and there was no point in employing a temporary secretary while he wasn't there. My stomach sank. Here I was unemployed again. Bad as the job was, at least it was paying me.

"But, we may have something more suited to you," said the agent. "An orthopaedic consultant at another hospital is looking for a good secretary with orthopaedic experience. It's at a nice modern hospital in Chelsea, they tell me."

"Okay."

"Can you start tomorrow? It's only a temporary post at present, but it should last for at least one year."

It sounded good, I thought, but it was best not to get my hopes up. When I got home that night, a letter lay on the mat from the local hospital. The previous week I had applied for a job as bed manager with them. Now they were asking me to report for an interview the following morning. So once again I was in a predicament. Which should I go for?

Fortunately, my interview was scheduled for 9.30 am, so I took a chance. I decided to be honest. I rang the London hospital, explained my dilemma and promised that hopefully, I would be able to make it to London for 11 am. They were extremely understanding.

My local interview went brilliantly. Boy could I bluff when I needed to. But deep inside I knew that I could do any of those jobs with my eyes closed. All I needed was to get my foot in the door and then I could show them. They were delighted with me and made no secret of the fact that I was just what they were looking for.

"If we were to offer you the job, how soon could you start?" they inquired.

"How about yesterday," I gushed silently.

Then I was off out the door followed by a mad dash to London. By 11.30 am I was installed in my plush new office high above the streets of Kensington and Chelsea. I thought I had landed in heaven.

"You are just what we need," they informed me. "A good mature orthopaedic PA. Not some young fly-by-night that only turns up every other day, like we've had for the past six months. If there is anything you need, don't hesitate to ask."

I went home that night on a cloud of joy once again. But this time I was cautious. I had been to this point only two weeks earlier, and this time I was taking nothing for granted.

Next morning, I got a call saying that I was being offered the job of bed manager at the local hospital in Surrey. Could I start on Monday? What do they say about waiting hours for a bus and then they all come together? Quandary. Quandary. Which should I take? I had the option of working in a rural hospital in Surrey, possibly getting into a boring rut, or instead, I had the prospect of an exciting job in London, in a large new hospital, amidst all the hustle and the bustle of the big city, and starting a new life for myself. Maybe even taking up where I had left off thirty years earlier. Which job do you think I took?

6

Just One More

*B*ack in the early days, I had not taken seriously my husband's love of being in either the bookies or the pub at every opportunity. Like any young wife and mother, I presumed it was just a phase and that he would grow out of it before too long. Besides, it was nice for him to be able to spend his hard-earned salary on enjoying himself. And there was always enough left over for the kids and myself. He was very kind to us and always insisted that the children and I go to the pub and the bookies with him on his afternoons off work.

Still, sitting on a bar stool with a small baby on my knee, and two toddlers at my feet, drinking G&Ts that I did not want at 4 pm on a Thursday or a Saturday afternoon, made me feel that I was not perhaps being a very good parent. The smoky boozy confines of a small dark pub was no place for young innocents. As the months crept by, it was no longer the norm to leave and go home at 6 pm.

'Just one more' became the phrase in fashion. The toddlers were becoming more and more tired and irritable and the baby was developing a smoker's cough. Eventually, I began to leave for home on my own, with Daddy following an hour later. Then it became two hours later, then three, then four, then 1 am in the morning. Someone had to start giving our children a home, and I seemed to be the only one interested. Eventually, on his half days, it was a direct journey from work to the pub, via the bookies.

Yet my husband was a wonderful doctor, loved and admired by all his patients. He gave them his all. He had compassion for them. He spent time with them. He listened to them. He held their hands while they were dying. Even as a young intern, he had sat with my father throughout his last agonising hours, in an effort to make his death from cancer more bearable. Not an easy job.

He gave so much of himself to his patients, that there was nothing left over. He was never a phone call or doorbell away from them. When not on duty, the only comfort he desired was a drink. This was his only solace. The responsibility of a family was too much to deal with, so he blotted it out with alcohol. Then, it was back on duty as usual.

Home did not enter the picture, except to phone and say, "I've just dropped in for one." One or twenty-one. It really didn't matter what the intention was. The result was always the same – 1 am became 2, then 3, then 4 and eventually 8 am.

We went out together at weekends and came home together to let the babysitter go at midnight. But then there was an insistence on driving the babysitter home, even though she only lived a hundred yards away. Then disappearance. He didn't came back until the next morning, and eventually, until the next afternoon.

"Don't you know what he's doing?" said a drunken acquaintance one late night in a noisy bar in 1978.

"Surely you know, Marguerite. You must know who he is with every night."

The acquaintance derived great pleasure in filling me in on the gory details. I could see it in his beady eyes. It was New Year's Eve and I was far from home with a group of friends. My husband had declined the invitation to join us. Immediately, I could feel the blood freeze in my veins. I could feel the hot sweat break out all over my body. The jigsaw fell into place with a resounding crash. The train came roaring out of the tunnel. I had no place to run. No place to hide. No way to make it all go away. The ugly truth. I was twenty-eight-years-old, with three small children, and my husband was having an affair with a local barmaid. Everyone knew about it but me. Ha! Ha! Ha! The stupid wife.

The feeling in the pit of my stomach on that night was one I was to experience many times over in the following twenty years. I was to discover that not alone was my husband addicted to alcohol and gambling, but he was also addicted to adultery. Hampered by this triple addiction, did our marriage ever really stand a chance?

And then suddenly for a brief two-year period in the early 1980s our lives were bliss. The long-awaited sobriety, which was to change our lives completely, finally arrived.

"It's so wonderful to wake up feeling great every morning," he assured me as he smiled at us all.

Our lives took on a previously unknown happiness. The stomach ulcer that had crippled me for the previous five years began to heal. The children smiled and laughed every day, as their father played with them, helped with their homework, and took them to all the places they loved.

He and I began to do everything together once more. We had money for the first time ever since our marriage. We planned the building of a new house together. That Christmas, he told me it was the first one he had enjoyed in years. And most important of all, we had our second honeymoon. A real honeymoon this time with two glorious blissful weeks in Cyprus. I felt like I was on another planet. He was so relaxed and we were so happy together that I had to pinch myself just to make sure I wasn't dreaming. Then one day, it all stopped.

"I've just called in for one. I'll be home shortly."

The blood froze in my veins and the ulcer bit into my intestines. Over the next three months, I stood by helplessly as he slipped slowly back down into that dark hole out of my reach. Only this time it was even more painful. This time, we had tasted a little bit of heaven and knew what it could be like.

7

Road to Recovery

"We will open the meeting this evening with a reading from September 4th," Mary announced. "This tells us about coming to believe that there is a power greater than ourselves."

I felt my throat constricting. What was I doing there? My God, how had I ever let my friend talk me into coming to Al-Anon? I must have been off my head. How could those strangers possibly know what was going on in my life?

They all looked so calm. Some even looked happy. I didn't know why *they* could be there. I decided to make an excuse and leave after ten minutes. The sooner I was out of there, the better! But they then pulled all the chairs into a large circle and everyone looked very cosy.

"But we've some new members tonight," Mary continued. "So maybe we should all introduce ourselves to start off with."

Around the circle they started. I'm Christine. I'm Patsy. I'm Jane. Tony. Catherine. Carol. The names went on.

"I'm Ruth," said the woman sitting next to me.

Here goes. My turn.

"I'm Marguerite," I croaked.

I hardly recognised the sound of my own voice. Instead, I could feel the sweat on my palms and the heat on my face. I barely registered those other names after my own. Relief flooded through me. I had actually managed to open my mouth without anyone thinking I was foolish. A huge surge of relief spread through me.

"Okay, that's everyone. Right, now we'll start the reading."

The reading began and I tried to concentrate, but I really hadn't a clue what it was all supposed to mean – 'higher power', 'let go and let God', 'courage to change', 'serenity'. What on earth was all that? Let go? Let bloody go, I thought! How in the name of God could I have let go? Wasn't that the biggest problem? In fact, I had to hang on so tight to everything and everyone in my family. Christ, if I had let go, then he would really have gone out of control and our whole miserable world fallen apart. What a load of waffle, I thought.

Then the 'courage to change' bit. Wasn't that what I had been trying to do for years. Change him. Change him into a respectable husband and father instead of a drunk. I didn't need some book and a bunch of people telling me I had to change things. The only thing that needed changing was James, and he had downright refused to do that. As far as he was concerned, there was no problem. After a while, my head had started to spin from all this talk.

"Okay, now we'll go around the room and say what our week has been like," said Mary.

She glanced around and nodded at a dark-haired woman, sitting across from me.

"Ann, can we start with you this week?" she suggested.

"Right," Ann replied.

Ann coughed a little nervously and shifted slightly in her chair.

"Well, I've had a not-too-bad week really, considering," she began. "I found the meeting last week particularly helpful, and…I related a lot to what Pat had said about her situation and about controlling. Like most of us, I was under the impression that if I didn't watch my husband every minute, then something absolutely terrible would happen to us all. I lost sight of the fact that Paddy is a grown man and must take responsibility for his own life…I'd been afraid to do this, so he sailed by knowing I'd be there at every turn, to pick up the pieces…

So I had to let him face up to some of the consequences of his behaviour."

Ann paused for breath, then continued.

"This happened on Sunday last. Up to now, I had always covered up for him with our friends and parents, even his boss. Part of me felt that if I let them see him in his worst condition, then it would somehow be a reflection on me. Was I not able to make him happier or whatever? All the usual things, we imagine people will say," she said, looking around as the group nodded in agreement.

"Anyway, his parents were due to call round on Sunday...Then he started to turn nasty, saying, 'At least if you came with me to the pub, then I wouldn't have to stay half as long.' I was about to give in and take the kids with me...But I remembered what I'd heard here last week...I'm not going to lie for you anymore...I'm not going to pretend...He came back four hours later, well jarred... 'I'm fine,' he says. 'Just because I had a couple of pints you have to go all high and mighty...just fuck off and leave me alone.'...He stripped off his clothes...just his boxer shorts...eventually he fell asleep on the couch, which at least shut him up...On Monday, he blamed it all on me...Anyway, that's all, and thanks everyone," she quickly concluded.

"Thank you for that Ann, and I'm sure we can all identify with your feelings. You acted well by giving Paddy some responsibility for his own actions. Kate, would you like to go next?

"Thanks, Mary," said Kate. "I haven't had a great week really. I..."

I didn't hear any more after that. I sat there in a state of shock. Ann had just talked about my family. She had told my story exactly. Her husband was out of control. I understood the feeling exactly. Her husband's drinking had been ruling their lives. My God, I thought, maybe she really understood. Maybe, I thought, if I stayed till the end of the meeting, I might get a chance to talk to her for a minute, before I dashed home again to whatever catastrophe lay waiting for me. But I also had to rush home in case he found out where I'd been. He would have killed me if he knew.

"Marguerite, is there anything you would like to share with us on what you're feeling at the moment?" Mary then asked. "We know what it's like on the first night, so if you'd prefer to pass this time, that would be fine."

"Emm, thanks. Eh, I don't know really. I just feel..." I replied.

I swallowed very hard. I felt a lump the size of a watermelon in my throat. My eyes had begun to sting and fill up with liquid. Please God, don't let me cry, I had screamed at myself. Please don't let me lose my dignity in front of these people, I implored.

A hush had descended on the room. There wasn't a sound. Just silence. But not an embarrassing silence. It was more like a warm gentle comforting embrace. It was enveloping me and making me feel safe.

"I just feel, so...so exhausted in my head from trying to cope," I began. "It seems that no matter what I do, he just keeps drinking and drinking and getting worse every time. I...I just feel like I'm going to crack up, if I don't get help. I...just feel...so useless. I'm letting my children down, even letting him down because I can't do anything to help him. He can't seem to see what he's doing to himself, and to the children. I..."

Then I started to sob. Great big gulping sobs. I felt as though a dam had burst inside me and all the tears that had been stored up for years had come gushing out in torrents. Some kind soul put a box of tissues into my hand, and another put a comforting hand on my shoulder. They let me cry. No, they allowed me to cry. No one said, "Oh, stop that stupid crying and feeling sorry for yourself, you stupid useless woman." They just sat and waited until I had regained my composure.

"Well, Marguerite, you're in the right place now, if you want to look for help. That is what this group is all about," Mary responded. "Just remember, the person you are here for is you, yourself. The only person you can change is yourself. Only you have that power. Then as you begin to change, possibly those around you may begin to change with you."

It was on that day in 1985 when I learned to stop trying to change my husband. I still remember the little card I had been given to read. *God grant me the serenity to accept the things I cannot change, the courage to change the things I can, and the wisdom to know the difference.* Thus began the first step in *my* long road to recovery, with many gaping potholes along the way.

8

Settling In

In London, my son and I became quite contented in our rented flat as the months went by. At first, it had been extremely difficult to become acclimatized to the strange surroundings and the strain of getting up at 6 am to get to work and school on time. Luke took refuge and security in my bed on the majority of nights and after a couple of months, I began to relax a little.

One snag was that I had told the owners that I did not have any children. The reason being that children are not allowed in many rented properties in London. They did mention, however, that grandchildren were allowed to visit. In view of this, I sneaked my son in and out each day, telling him to call me 'Granny' if anyone else was listening. I tried as much as possible to make it into a game with him, where we were on a secret mission and had to keep our identities hidden. He quite enjoyed it actually.

The majority of the residents in this block of flats were retired couples or middle-aged matrons. Few of them had the ability to smile or to say hello. If any of them asked, I would pretend that Luke was visiting. My contract clearly stated *No children or pets*. Actually, pets were probably more acceptable than children!

Gradually, we settled in and he was finally able to have his friends for a sleepover occasionally. On these occasions my nerves were in tatters. Trying to keep four nine-year-old boys quiet in such a setting was not easy. One of them, in particular, was wired to the National

Grid and needed continuous supervision. I slept one night with an eye constantly open, I do recall.

This was also my first experience ever of not being able to park my car outside my own front door. In fact, it was also the first time in years that I did not actually possess 'my own front door'. It is strange how we take such basics in life for granted.

Did I ever imagine in all the years that I complained about dragging loaded shopping bags from my car to the kitchen, that I would one day end up hauling heavy bags from the opposite side of a busy main road, down a pathway and up three flights of stairs, just to get to the door of my flat? It was an exhausting process, and one that left me gasping for breath on many occasions. I soon learnt that it was best to shop in small quantities, although this in itself was a nightmare as it meant having to join the long supermarket queues after work almost every second evening.

Through that long hot summer I longed for my garden. I longed to go out and potter about among the shrubbery and train the clematis up along the fences. I had been growing *Clematis montana*, my favourite, for years, wherever we had lived. Now I imagined how it was looking on the side of my house in Donegal, with its pretty pink flowers spreading further and further over fences and walls. Who would be there to tend it this time? I longed to sit in the back garden and read my book and listen to the radio, as I had done in the past. Now I had no back garden. Not even a back yard. There was a communal garden of sorts, but the thoughts of climbing up and down three flights of stairs to get to it, took some of the enthusiasm out of the exercise.

Most of all, I missed my piano. All my life, I had played on a succession of old second-hand pianos. I had always promised myself that if I could ever afford it, I would buy myself a shining new one. A year earlier, following my mother's death, I fulfilled that promise and bought a beautiful new piano with part of my small inheritance. The previous Christmas, one of my sons had given me the entire collection of Beethoven Piano Concertos on CD. As I listened to them, I set myself the challenge of learning to play my two favourite sonatas by the end of that year. I had bought the sheet music and had set myself two hours of practice each day. Now all that work was going to waste, as I had no means to keep up my practice, and my lovely piano lay idle in a locked room in Donegal. What a waste, I thought.

Looking back now, I see how we lived as paupers in those months. I was so afraid to spend the few pounds I had that sometimes I practically starved us. In addition, I had us living without the usual trappings that most of the western world today take for granted, like a decent TV for instance. I am not a great TV viewer, but my young son had been used to having Sky with all its trimmings on a twenty-eight-inch screen.

What he had to adjust to now was laughable. In my rush to leave Donegal, I had taken a small portable TV for him. I had actually bought it second-hand fifteen years earlier. It picked up the four basic stations so at least that was something. However, the remote control had somehow got damaged en route so we had no way of altering the volume, which was stuck on 'very low'. Inaudible, in fact. My son-in-law came to our rescue one day when I found him heading for the local dump with an old TV from his student days. It had sound but no picture, he told me. Brilliant, I thought. We can team the two together. We can have sound on one and a picture on the other. And so we spent our nights, with our twin TVs side by side. Again, my son never complained and I was past caring. Sometimes he would say, "Mum, can we get a proper TV when we buy our new house?" This was what kept him going. Each weekend as we drove around the area, he would see 'House for Sale' signs everywhere.

"Can we buy that one?" he would ask over and over.

"Maybe," was always my answer. Well, no point in crushing his dreams. He had to have something to cling to.

All pleas to my husband for an extension to my 'allowance' fell on deaf ears. He had absolutely no idea of the actual cost of day-to-day living, having never been involved in such issues over the years. He had no concept of the myriad extras that a mere child can incur during the course of one school week. One day, in desperation, I rang a particular colleague of my husband's in Donegal, whom I thought might be able to sway his mind. Perhaps he could convince my husband that the costs of bringing up a young boy on what I was earning was becoming increasingly difficult with each passing week.

"Could you not send the wee lad back and let one of Jimmy's sisters raise him for you?" he suggested instead.

I was speechless. I was shocked. I was disgusted. I was extremely angry. How, in today's modern Ireland could anyone see a young child as a simple commodity? Was this perhaps how some men looked on children? Some fifty years earlier, in post-war Ireland, my mother had helped out with the rearing of one of her nephews from an extremely large family, when the child's mother became unwell. But I thought we had moved on a lot since then. Nine years earlier, on the day our little boy came into the world, I had promised him that I would be there for him, to love and protect him for as long as I could manage to live. The thought of handing him over to someone else to do that job for me was so alien, that I almost felt physically sick.

"To raise the child for you," he repeated.

What was Luke? A young dog, whose owners found him a bit difficult to control in the city, so they were sending him to an uncle in the country to run about the farm instead. And what about the child himself? Would he not feel just slightly abandoned by his mother? Had he not been abandoned by enough people in his life already? Would he not miss his mother? Would his mother not miss him? I just found the suggestion totally astounding.

Then one day in work, I thought I had found the answer to all my problems. Someone in the office mentioned rent allowance and child benefit allowance for single parents. My heart leapt with glee. The wonderful DHSS, the Department of Health & Social Services whose path I had encountered when looking for a flat in my first week in England, might now be about to save my life, well financially anyway. I got on the phone straightaway and discovered that I could possibly be eligible for a gigantic windfall. It was even hinted over the phone from the DHSS office that I might get over half my rent paid every month. I was delirious with excitement.

The following day the application forms arrived in the post. Over those fourteen pages I was to divulge every single detail about myself, my son, my marriage, my income. How much did I spend on this? How much did I spend on that? Nothing was private. I had to measure each of the rooms, and state what I used them for. I didn't know what to say about my son, in case the DHSS contacted the owner and gave my game away. If I didn't claim for him, then I wouldn't be eligible. If I did claim for him, we might lose the flat. I had no one to turn to for advice. But I didn't care anymore. There was nothing left for me to do. I had to claim benefit from the state. But I was scared. I was even scared that if I gave incorrect information, they could throw me in prison. This fear of prison was with me all through my first couple of years in England. I was constantly looking over my shoulder. The law terrified me.

Eventually six weeks later, I received notification from the DHSS that an inspector would call to my flat to interview me and check out my living conditions. I felt sick. What if they accused me of fraud? But then, I hadn't lied on the form, so what was I afraid of? But I was still sick with worry. I cleaned and tidied the flat. Then I messed it up again. Then I tidied it again. I wasn't sure what to do. If it looked too good, the inspector would not feel sorry for me. If it looked too bad, they would think I was an unfit mother.

Finally the inspector arrived. He was a nice man but I felt naked. He knew everything about me and that left me with very little pride. After introducing himself, he explained that he would have to look around the flat. With that, he proceeded to open all wardrobes, drawers, cupboards, look under beds and behind chairs. Was he checking to see if I had hidden any valuable family heirlooms? I should be so lucky. I felt my stomach heaving and a cold sweat breaking out. I wanted to cry but I couldn't let him see me.

Eventually, he left after searching into every nook and cranny of my life. I'm sure I'm not alone in feeling that one's bedroom is their private haven. It is a place that is out of bounds to all, but family. Maybe I was oversensitive, but I felt violated in a strange sort of way. I was willing to endure it, however, if it meant that we would have some financial relief.

Over the next ten weeks, I waited and I waited. We were so sure that we would be getting a huge rebate.

"When we get the rent money, Mum, can I get a skateboard?" Luke asked.

"When we get the rent money, Mum, can I get new football boots?"

Everyday, we planned what we would do with the money. We would pay off all our outstanding bills and then have some sort of a treat for ourselves. Maybe a day out in London. The thoughts of this cheque kept us going for a long time.

Eventually, following constant telephone inquiries and constant promises that a cheque was in the post, I got a letter stating that I did not qualify for benefit as my income was just above the limit. We were gutted. I was advised, however, that if I were to give up work and move to a rundown area on the other side of town, then I would qualify for rent allowance and child benefit combined.

Setbacks like this constantly left me in tatters. It seemed that each time I thought I was making some headway, I ran into another brick wall. Unfortunately, I had promised my son a decent TV once this windfall would land on our mat. Now I had let him down as well and all of that humiliation had been for nothing. Just for a brief period that day I considered the option of giving up work, but I knew that I would go under completely if I did not have my work to keep me busy. I also needed to hang on to whatever bit of dignity I had left.

Instead I focussed on the little things in life that gave me most pleasure. I took up yoga classes and it opened up a whole new world for me. Another joy was the area in which my work was situated. Kensington and Chelsea are the most beautiful parts of London in my eyes. I love the beauty of the old architecture, the tree-lined roads, the beautiful little parks and the fabulous antique shops. Each morning as I made the twenty-minute walk between South Kensington Station and my office, I entered a type of dream world. I imagined that I lived in one of those beautiful elegant buildings. As I passed, I looked in the windows of the various drawing rooms, with their lofted ceilings and the elegant decor on the walls and doors. I would try to imagine the people who had lived there a hundred years earlier, with their period gowns and hairstyles. I imagined the footmen and the carriages on the cobbled streets. Sometimes I imagined meeting a handsome Prince Charming who would come and rescue me from my flat and take me to live with him in such a beautiful setting.

Some mornings, if I timed it right, I was accompanied along the Fulham Road by a troop of the Queen's horses, on exercise from the nearby Chelsea barracks. It was an unforgettable sight at 7 am on a summer's morning, with the early sunshine glistening on the flanks of those beautiful examples of equine perfection. It was times like this that my spirits soared and I thanked God for giving me the opportunity of being there. The odd thing was that I had actually lived in one of these grand mansions in my past, albeit briefly. During my time in London in the summer of '68, that part of London was going through an entirely different phase. The modern architecture of the sixties had the rich and famous clamouring for modern buildings – those gross monstrosities that can be seen in many cities all over Europe. Georgian, Edwardian and Victorian London became undesirable. People wanted glass and lots of it. And so it was that the area around south Kensington contained hundreds and thousands of cheap bedsits. One big drawing room converted into a flat for two or three or more. What did one care so long as they had beds, a few chairs, the use of a kitchen and, of course, a shared bathroom? We had lived in one of these houses for a week before going back to Galway and as we passed the modern buildings that were mushrooming in the surrounding areas, we had been envious. But the rent in those high-rise places was colossal. Now life had reversed itself and Georgian London was the place-to-be again.

Another positive thing about living in London was the changes it brought to me as a person. Having to run my life to such a strict regime was probably one of the best things that ever happened to me. It made me extremely organised. I got things done so much faster. It was a whole new experience for me. For the first years of my marriage, I didn't have the opportunity to take on a full-time job. I had always wanted to, but circumstances had prevented it happening. There were many factors involved.

Number one, I suppose, was that I had three small children. This in itself, however, should never stop any woman from working outside the home.

Number two, however, was more important. We had been forced to live a totally erratic lifestyle. My husband worked in an extremely busy GP practice in Donegal, along with two partners. He was, however, totally disorganised. I never knew from one day to the next, if he was on call, not on call, working or not working. I never knew when I would be up all night answering the phone to patients, or to the local Garda station when they needed a doctor to take blood tests in drink driving cases. On occasions too numerous to mention, neither of us got more than two or three hours sleep at night.

My husband's personal lifestyle was also totally erratic. He was of the firm opinion that the children were my responsibility and mine only. His lifestyle did not make room for dropping children at elocution or picking them up from dancing class. Homework was my responsibility, as well as tucking them up in bed for the night. During those years, I tried working for a year teaching music, but soon found that my children were losing out too much and the strain becoming unbearable. There was no support in looking after them.

So I stopped and put my career and my ambitions on the back burner. I did, however, teach children's piano lessons in my own home over the years, but this was not like a 'real job'. I did not have to get dressed up and put my make-up on and leave the house by a certain time. Instead my work came to me. I enjoyed this period of my life, but it did not satisfy my appetite to be out there in the workplace, making my mark.

The third reason I did not work was that my husband was extremely set against it. When I did eventually get myself re-trained for the workplace in 1991 to get a full-time job, he was 110 per cent against it. I was told that my place was at home, looking after my son and not leaving him to strangers to look after for me. But I persisted as I loved my newfound opportunity to progress. I placed my son with a wonderful childminder, who treated him just like her own. He adored her then and still does to this day.

Now I was working in London and feeling very proud of myself. I even began to dream about buying a little place of our own some day, and not having to worry about landlords.

9

Breakthrough

It was 1989 when the trouble really started. Our beautiful baby boy Luke had arrived a year earlier and we were deriving immense enjoyment from his presence. However, there was one major fly in the ointment. My husband's drinking had once again escalated out of control and was beginning to take over every aspect of our lives. This time, my children were my main concern. The two eldest were due to sit their Leaving Cert exams that June, and were studying very hard. Or trying to, I should say.

However, their father had added a new dimension to his behaviour. At this stage in their lives, they had begun to accept that when in drinking mode, he rarely came home, at least not until very late at night or early the next morning. He might possibly even stay away for a few days, depending on his form.

However, during the months of January and February, he had taken to coming home drunk around 4.30 or 5 pm each afternoon. This was driving us mad, as he would come in, stagger about, talking through his hat, and then proceed to wander in and out of the kids' bedrooms, where they had already begun to study. This messing and looking for an argument would go on until maybe 7 pm, and by this stage everyone was so much on edge that no study was possible. The atmosphere in the house was terrible. I would try to entice him to go to bed for a few hours, or to sit and eat something, or even God forbid, go back to the pub again. But nothing would shift him. He dug himself in.

One evening we were pushed to the brink. When we saw his car pull up in the driveway, we made a hasty decision to lock him out. It was

4.15 pm and we had all taken enough. He came to the patio doors of the kitchen-cum-living room and we could see from the swaying and stumbling that he was well cooked. He tried to slide the door open. He seemed confused when it did not budge. We stood inside and I explained to him that he could not come in as he was preventing the kids from studying. We were all tired of it. I suggested that he go sleep it off in the car. He shouted and roared. And as on many previous occasions I was on the verge of giving in. I felt very sorry for him, but we could not let it go on. I had to be strong.

Eventually, I told the kids to go to their books and try to do some studying. After some time, I left the room and went to get on with my work, when I heard very loud banging coming from the living room area. Some thirty minutes later, he was still banging. I pleaded with him to stop and leave us alone, but he was resolute.

We hoped that he would eventually get so tired that he would give up. But he didn't, and ten minutes later, the carpet was littered with shards of broken glass. He was in. And he was red with fury. He sat in the midst of the glass, in the armchair, watching TV as though it were the most natural situation in the world, then got up, walked out through the door and drove off. That was the end of study for another day.

He arrived back one hour later and I then took the decision to call a friend of his, an ex-Garda. I asked him to call to the house to show him what had happened. He came and spoke to him and then took him away for the rest of the evening until he sobered up. The next day, the older children and I took the decision that I should visit an out-of-town solicitor and seek a barring order against my husband. It was the only thing left for us to do. We could not go on like this.

The solicitor was very understanding, but asked that he might be allowed to speak to my husband before proceeding with the barring order. I passed on this information to my husband along with the details of what was about to happen, and he agreed to the meeting.

Well he had no choice really. It was either talk to the solicitor or he was out. It had come to that. Whatever that solicitor said to him, it worked. He went on the wagon.

10

'A Very Saleable Commodity'

As the weeks wore on, James managed to stay off the booze and life was good again. We all began to relax and the atmosphere in the house was great. Once again we began to make plans. This was always the way in periods of abstinence.

In mid-May some people came and asked him if he would be interested in running in the general election three weeks later. When he told us that evening after work, our first thought was "Aha, he's been drinking again." But he was serious.

"They want me to run for Fianna Fáil in the general election," he said.

"Who are 'they'?" one of us asked.

He mentioned some names, most of whom I had heard of in the past, but I was unaware that they were in any way politically involved. We all agreed it was a crazy idea. As he said himself, he knew nothing about politics, and wouldn't even know where to start.

The following evening he was back with the same story. 'They' had contacted him again and were putting pressure on him to say yes.

"But what would it mean?" we asked.

"What would you have to do?"

"Well, basically just go to Dublin two or three days a week really."

"Would you get paid for it?" I asked.

"I think so," he replied.

This goes to show just how little our family knew about politics.

As the election would be taking place in the middle of the exams, we all agreed that it would not be a good time to be fooling around with something like this and that it was best to say no. But next day, there was more pressure.

"You get a salary of £27,000 a year for it," he informed us. "And you only have to go to Dublin for about thirty weeks of the year."

"Well, I suppose, that isn't too bad," I said. "We could definitely do with the extra money to pay off all those loans and overdrafts in the bank."

But still we were not convinced.

The next evening as I was about to leave the house for my night class at 7.30 pm, the phone rang.

"Hello, is that Dr McDaid's home?" I was asked.

"Yes it is," I replied.

"Can you hold for a call please from Mr Haughey in Leinster House?"

"Hello, Charles Haughey here," a voice announced.

What? Who? I almost dropped the receiver.

"Could I speak to your husband please, Mrs McDaid?"

The sweet gravely tones came down the line and I thought I was listening to a radio presenter. No one of such importance had ever spoken to me before. I was frozen to the spot. God, I hoped my father was watching up in heaven. But then I could feel a huge laugh building up inside me. Was some joker having me on? No. The voice was genuine. With my composure totally regained, I managed to call my husband to the phone. And that was it. The call had come, directly from the top, from Il Duce himself, and we were in.

Yes, he would stand for Fianna Fáil.

Yes, he would pledge himself to the party.

Yes, he would lay down his life for the party.

Yes, he would pledge the lives of each family member for the party, even if he didn't know it at the time.

It was all quite exciting really. All the canvassing, all the meetings, all the chatting and the predicting. Yet for me, my main priority had to be my children and the important exams that were looming large, and which would dictate their future paths in life. They had both applied for university places with high point requirements and had always worked hard. It would be unfair to abandon them now. They needed regularity in their lives. They needed nourishing meals cooked. They needed peace and quiet. My husband was out of the house from 8 am until 2 am each day and night attending meetings, addressing rallies, having his photo taken. It was a pity, because while he had been sober during the previous four weeks, it had been nice to have him home more often, and we were just beginning to get on well together, minus the booze.

But still we reckoned, once the election was over we could get back to that way once again. For a start, the likelihood of him getting elected was minimal. First time out, no previous political experience, no history of County or Urban Council membership. But, on the other hand, he could smile brilliantly and look even cuter than Tony Blair when the need arose. 'A very saleable commodity' was how his election managers described him.

And so the people voted. And lo and behold, enough of them voted for the new kid on the block and he was elected. It was bedlam. When his name was called out, he leapt over a table and bounded onto the stage like *Red Rum* at Beecher's Brook. He looked so wonderful that night, so invigorated and so strong, and I felt so proud of him. The kids and myself were in bits. We were so happy for him. The tears of joy welled in our eyes. All around us the crowds were cheering and shouting. Everyone was hugging and kissing. We had never seen anything like it before. It was a truly wonderful and happy time. In the bar later on that night, people came to me and said, "Enjoy your last few hours as a private citizen."

"Things will be different now. He's public property now, you know."

I hadn't got a clue what they were talking about. I was just looking forward to getting a chance to talk to him in the following weeks, and find out about what had been happening.

Next day was spent touring the constituency in a 'cavalcade', thanking the voters. All new to us again, but tremendously exciting. We were still on a high from the previous day's events. I managed to speak to him for a couple of brief minutes that day. The next day, Sunday, there were more phone calls, and reporters and photographers at the house all day. Then on Monday, he was whisked off to Dublin to be introduced to Leinster House. He came back the following day with boxes of free envelopes. All prepaid. Now what were we possibly going to do with all those hundreds of envelopes? Naive or what?

Next day, he was back to work in his medical practice. He arrived home for lunch accompanied by advisors. No chance to talk to him. Over lunch, he was taught how to reply to queries from constituents.

"You will get a lot of people coming to you looking for things," they said.

What sort of things? I wondered.

"Once they get your phone number, you'll probably get some calls to the house," they informed us.

Oh well, the odd phone call won't bother me too much, I mused. We had become used to being disturbed at all hours of the day and night with patients calling.

Two weeks later, the entire family decamped to Dublin, where outside Leinster House, the sun was shining and the air filled with excitement. All around us the raw new TDs and their families posed for happy photographs. It was like something from another world. My God, who would have ever thought that we would be on this hallowed ground?

Inside, we watched proudly from the visitor's gallery as he took his seat in the chamber. I wondered what was going through his mind at that moment. My father would be so proud of him, I thought silently to myself. But I was sure he was watching from above, somewhere.

Afterwards, we were introduced to the sanctum of the Dáil Bar and to that other metropolis of politics, Buswell's Hotel, just across the street. It's strange really. We had been in Dublin hundreds of times before, but never aware of any of these places before that day. We didn't even know where Leinster House was. But like anyone not involved in politics, we never had a need to know, I suppose. And that, shall we say, was that. Life changed utterly.

Six months earlier, I had booked a holiday to Spain for the family, and we were due to leave shortly after the end of the Leaving Cert. We were all looking forward to relaxing and spending some time together. As it turned out, the kids and myself trooped off to Spain on our own in July, as the political leaders in Dublin had difficulty in forming a government, and my husband was unable to leave the country until they got their act together. A huge disappointment to us all, but there would be other times we hoped. Wrong again.

That was thirteen years ago, and since then I never got an opportunity to sit down and speak to him. There was never any time. Family matters, financial matters, personal matters. Everything disappeared out the window in those first few weeks, never to get to the top of the agenda ever again. He had been given a job to do and by God, he was going to do it well. No one would ever get the opportunity to criticise his work rate. He would sacrifice all in pursuit of adoration and applause.

With our home doubling as a 'political office' as well as a 'medical surgery', it was soon turned into a public highway. I remember getting home from work one cold December evening at 5.30 pm after collecting my son from the childminder. We were both tired and hungry. The house was full of people. In the kitchen, some people waited for advice on housing grants. In the living room, a couple waited for their passports queries to be sorted out. A man in the surgery waited for an injection. In the study, a deputation waited for a meeting about a grant for a new school. In the hallway, my husband was having simultaneous telephone conversations, holding a mobile phone in one hand and the house phone in the other. As he was always unwilling to accept my offers of help with his work, I took my son upstairs and we sat in the bedroom doing homework until the kitchen became free and I could start preparing dinner.

Weekends were much worse. One evening I was getting ready to go out, and came downstairs from the shower, clad in nothing but a towel. I presumed I was alone in the house, as Luke was outside playing. Just as I reached the bottom step, a strange man popped his head out of my living room.

"I'm looking for the political office," he said. "Is this it?"

He had just opened the front door and let himself in.

When I look back on it now, I ask myself, what if there was no incident back in 1989? What if he hadn't got six weeks sobriety behind him when approached by the heavy mob? He couldn't have handled the election. The past thirteen years would then have never happened. Funny how the little decisions we make in life have the greatest effect on our futures. Maybe we should have unlocked the door, let him in and let him keep on drinking. At least then, we would have had a husband and a father.

11

Money Matters

$\mathcal{E}$very morning when I woke up in London, my first thought was money. There was just not enough to go round. I was continuously worrying about it. I had the terrifying fear that I would get into debt and the police would throw me into prison. I know it sounds totally daft, but for me it was a distinct possibility.

Then one day my solicitor in Dublin rang me at my office in London. Halfway through our conversation he happened to mention something.

"By the way, I presume you heard about the big win?"

"What big win? Whose big win?" I queried.

"Your husband's big win, of course. Sure it's all over the papers. He's supposed to have won £75,000 at Cheltenham last week."

"You're joking? Is it really true?"

"Well, he's not denying it. Although he claims that 75k is a bit of an exaggeration," he added.

After he hung up, I rang my daughter.

"Did you hear anything from Dad about him winning money at Cheltenham last week?" I asked her.

"No, I'm sure we're the last ones he'd tell, in case he had to give us some of it," she replied, tongue-in-cheek.

I then rang my son in Dublin. He had heard nothing from him either, but someone at work had mentioned that they had read about it in the paper. I told my young son the good news after school and he was thrilled. Maybe now Dad would get him the new computer game he had wanted for ages, I thought. I began to foolishly think that some of my husband's good fortune might even come my way. Silly me. Not many months after that, my daughter rang me to say that Dad had been awarded £90,000 compensation in a libel case in court. Once again, I allowed my hopes to rise. Well, I was a bit of a slow learner then.

Some months later, I was merrily told that the whole county, or even country, had been bought a drink, or maybe even two, on the strength of his double good luck. Perhaps the kids and myself should have come back for a night to Letterkenny, and you never know, he might even have bought us a drink too. As it was, we got zilch. According to my husband, it had all gone to charity! Now what is it about charity beginning at home? Or even beginning with a woman and child in a dingy flat in Surrey for that matter.

But then, money, or the lack of it, was always an issue with my husband. I could never approach him and ask him directly for money for what was needed. I always had to rehearse what I would say for days in advance, in an effort to prevent him flying into a rage. But I rarely succeeded.

My impecunious state in England brought back all the bitter arguments over money throughout the years. But it need not have been like that. My husband was a partner in one of the largest and most successful medical practices in the country. Most of his classmates and colleagues seemed to be able to afford big houses, big cars, expensive antiques, luxurious foreign holidays and still have some left over to invest in savings for their old age. Yet, we lived from year to year on the breadline. Our house was stocked with second-hand furniture, not antiques, just old cast-offs. I drove a second-hand car which broke down with annoying regularity. My husband's car was not much better. The house was dark and dreary. There was no money for painters or decorators. That was all left for me to do. It didn't matter what the kids or I needed money for, it was just never given without a begging struggle and a fight. And by the time it was grudgingly handed over to us, the good had been taken out of it. I think that's why I always wanted my own income, so that I would not have to beg for every single thing that my kids needed.

Of course, it hadn't always been that way. At the start he had been one of the most generous people I knew. Money never came into the conversation. It was never an issue. We shared everything. We did not need very much, except for drink. As long as we had enough for that we were happy. The few pints in the Skeff did not cost the earth when the crack was good. When we got married, he was still very generous and still shared everything. His mother and mine gave us money every month and my parents helped us out mostly with food and accommodation. Money was not a problem, even though we did not have very much. I didn't worry too much, I knew that the good times were ahead and once he got himself established in a good GP practice, money problems would be a thing of the past.

When my husband did eventually join a group medical practice, he ran his part of it as a charity. He refused offers of payment from his private patients. When they were treated at his Surgery, they were ushered out through the side door, thereby avoiding his secretary at her desk. When he saw patients at our home, I stood by helplessly and listened as patients pleaded with him.

"Here Jimmy, take a few pounds," one would say.

"Doctor, please take five pounds this time," said another.

All offers were met with, "No, no, I'm not taking anything from you."

A box of biscuits, a bottle of aftershave, or God forbid, a bottle of whiskey at Christmas was payment enough for him. Pretty low-cost medical care for an entire family for a full year, I should think. Meanwhile, behind the kitchen door, I would hide with teeth clenched and stomach tied in knots, knowing that when I asked for some extra housekeeping the following day, I would be roared at and shouted down.

However, as he began to drink more and more, the money did not stretch as far. When the children were born, they needed things, and this ate into the money, even though my mother took care of most of the clothes and the babysitting. Both our families were very good to us, financially and in every other way. Everyone helped really. I even managed to get us a job delivering newspapers to housing estates in Galway. We would get someone to look after the kids for a few hours and then dashed around to the houses. We were blessed. As the children grew, I was able to make all of their clothes, and most of my own too. I have two great photographs from that time. One taken of me in 1972 shows me wearing a pair of bell-bottom check trousers, with huge flares. The other photo taken in 1974 shows two little tots, both wearing matching dungarees of the same material. I had cut up the trousers and made an outfit out of each flared leg. Not bad going for a twenty-three-year-old wannabe hippie. All of their knitwear at that stage was made by my wonderfully talented mother-in-law. And all winter coats were made by my mother. However, as the children grew a little older, they began to need things that could not be sewn or knitted. By this time, my husband was earning a good wage, like all of his colleagues. Yet the money would never stretch for some reason. And then the kids started school.

New schoolbooks. Argument. Schoolbags. Argument. New winter shoes. Argument.

Anything they needed caused bad feeling. Children's allowance money was stashed away by me to cover birthdays so as not to cause another fight. Thursday was his half-day from work, so what else could he do only go to the pub and the bookie office? And Saturday was horse racing. The bookie was right next door to the pub. It was important that he be there. He was going to make his fortune with every pound he bet. Spend some time at home with the kids? Certainly not. No way. All they ever did was ask him for money! They could go to the pub with him if they liked. However, that novelty had long worn off.

"Every time I come in that front door, there's someone there with their hand out asking for money for this or that."

"Is it any wonder I don't come home?"

"This would drive any man to drink."

Then people would say to me, "I hear there was a big poker game in Sweeney's last Saturday night. I believe your fellow was betting in hundreds."

"Apparently, he was up £500 but then he lost it all and a lot more with it. I believe Joe Doherty made a killing. I'm surprised you allow your fellow to lose all that money."

Another time they said, "I hear your fellow had a big win in the bookies yesterday. Horse won at 30/1. He had £100 pounds on its nose."

I dashed home all excited.

"I hear you had a big win yesterday, how much did you get?" I gasped, out of breath.

I could see the bundle of notes bulging in his trouser pocket.

"About £500," was his reply.

"Brilliant," I said, knowing he was only acknowledging a small percentage of the amount. Still, never look a gift horse in the mouth. Better something than nothing. I had to tread carefully.

"Why don't we do something good with that money this time," I suggested meekly. "Like treat ourselves to something nice. Why not get yourself a nice new warm winter coat. That one you have for the past three years is getting a bit raggy and worn looking. You could do with a nice new one.

"And maybe, we could treat ourselves to a little weekend break or a coffee table for the sitting room," I continued. "That one I bought in the second-hand shop five years ago is a real eyesore, with all the scratches on it. I would really love just one nice piece of shiny new furniture, and not always have someone else's rejects. I saw a lovely one last week for only £49 in the furniture shop in town. It was on sale."

"You must be bloody joking," he retorted. "Every penny of that money is needed to pay off the bills you have mounted up on me. None of it will be going on luxuries."

I looked at him in disbelief.

"What do you think I am? Made of money? I'm going into town. I have to pay some bills. I'll be back later," he added as he walked off.

Three o'clock in the morning, I heard his car in the driveway. I listened through the open bedroom window, as he fumbled with his keys outside the front door below. Unable to find his door key, he eventually rang the bell. He'd lost it again. Third key that month. I climbed out of bed wearily and let him in. He could barely walk, he was so drunk. He then crawled upstairs and fell into bed. When he was unconscious, I sneaked out of bed and crawled around on my hands and knees to where he had left his trousers on the floor. Scarcely breathing, I inched my hand into the trouser pocket. Nothing there but a few loose one pound notes. Next I tried the other pocket, all the time keeping my eyes fixed on his face, in case he stirred. There it was, the bundle of bank notes. I removed them carefully from the pocket, noting exactly the way they were folded. I unrolled them slowly and started counting. One hundred, two hundred, three hundred and forty pounds. I wondered what he had done with the rest of the money if the bet had really been one hundred pounds at 30/1. Anyhow, since he left the house at 4 pm the previous evening, he had spent approximately one hundred and sixty pounds give or take a few pounds. But I knew when I would check later in the month that the ESB, the telephone or any other bills would not have been paid. However, some local barman and his family would be flying off to the Canaries for their winter holidays, thanks to the good graces of this man and his generosity in standing drinks to all the hangers-on in the local pub. And the bookmaker's wife would have another new coat this winter. Yet my children would still have to beg him for the price of a new school book.

As I was putting the money back, the thought occurred to me that in the morning, he might not remember how much he had spent the night before, and so maybe I could sneak a bit out of it for myself and the kids. It wasn't really stealing, I told myself. Wasn't it better that the children had it instead of the publican or bookmaker? It was all going to go to one or the other anyway. So I pulled the wad back out again. First I took out a twenty-pound note, and then put it back again. No, it wasn't right. What if he discovered it missing? I would have to lie. I didn't like lying. It was against my nature, against my conscience. But, this was in a good cause. I had to take the chance. With my heart thumping, I took out the note again. He stirred in the bed and I almost died of fright. I knelt there frozen to the spot, trying to think of what I would say if he rolled over and saw me. What excuse would I give for crawling around on my hands and knees at 3 am? If only I wore contact lenses, I could pretend that I had lost one on my way to the bathroom. Fortunately, he settled again.

I felt like a criminal as I crawled back into bed. Then I realised that I still had the money in my hand. My God, I had to hide it somewhere! Under the mattress was too obvious if he noticed it missing. Where then? I looked around the bedroom trying to spot somewhere that he would not think of looking. But there was nowhere. I sneaked out of bed again and went downstairs to the sitting room. I sat there thinking and looking around. Then I saw the perfect hiding place. My piano. He knew nothing about pianos, so he wouldn't be able to figure out how to get the front section removed to search in there. I turned the two wooden latches inside the top half, and removed this section. Then I lifted out the keyboard cover and placed my treasure inside the frame of the piano. Tucked in behind the strings. There I knew it would be safe. I sneaked back upstairs to bed and spent the remainder of the night lying awake, thinking about the terrible thing I had done. I had stolen from my own husband. I went over and over it in my mind, trying to rationalise it. Eventually, I fell into an exhausted sleep just five minutes before the alarm clock rang at 8 am.

The next day, he got up and got ready for work. I didn't even mention the money he had won, for fear of making him suspicious. Unfortunately, I had told the kids the previous evening that Daddy had won some money and that maybe he would give them a treat. Naturally, at breakfast they mentioned it to him. He told them that the money was for paying bills and not for wasting on them and their fancy ideas. He had a bad hangover and you could see in their eyes that the didn't want to push him too far. I got them organised for school and breathed a sigh of relief when they all went off with him in the car.

All day I made plans for the money. I wasn't going to touch it for at least two weeks, lest he became suspicious. I'd get the children what they'd been asking for and needed, but in such a way as not to make anyone wonder where I got the money. Especially him. I knew that by Saturday, all his winnings would be gone again. And really what he'd just won was only what he'd already put into the bookies for the previous month. He'd put a bet on anything that happened. Not just the horses and dogs.

This was where I learnt to start taking anything I could get for my family, before someone else got it. I was twenty-six-years-old and a thief.

12

London Season

One cold November afternoon in Surrey, when I had a day off work with a terrible head-cold, I received a phone call from Margaret Cahill, at that stage a total stranger to me. Margaret is a wonderful Irish woman and during the time I lived in London, she was the head of the Irish Tourist Board. My daughter and her husband were already on her mailing list for various events held annually to promote Ireland to the British.

"Would you like to attend a film premiere and reception as my guest?" she asked.

I was gobsmacked, to say the very least. Since my arrival in London several months earlier, I had literally not been outside the door after I arrived home from work at 7 pm. Now, here was someone inviting me to attend a social event. Naturally, my first inclination was to say no. Very definitely, no. Well, I didn't know anyone who was going. I didn't know what to wear. And even if I did, there was nothing in my wardrobe that would allow me out after dark. The only respectable item of clothing I possessed was my work suit from M&S.

But behind all of these excuses was the real one. I felt ugly, I felt useless, I felt like a piece of dirt on the street. My emotions were raw. My self-esteem was incredibly low, from exhaustion, from worry and from rejection. How could I possibly hold an intelligent conversation with a stranger, feeling like that?

But I could not let Margaret know this. One year earlier, I would have jumped at the chance and taken it in my stride. Margaret reassured me not to worry however.

"It'll be very enjoyable and I'll introduce you to lots of interesting people," she said.

I promised to ring her back in an hour, if I could get a babysitter. Any excuse, of course. I rang my daughter in a panic.

"What will I do?" I pleaded.

"Go on Mum, you'll be fine," she encouraged. "You love those kind of things. You'll have a great time."

So I said yes. Next evening I headed off, catching the train to London in an ancient black dress, salvaged from the depths of my daughter's wardrobe. It had come from St Bernard's emporium five years previously, but I dressed it up with some accessories so no one would be any the wiser. However, that evening the temperature was very low and I was frozen solid. At Victoria Station, I climbed the stairs to Molly O'Shea's, where I ordered a hot rum to thaw me out before heading off into the night to find a taxi. I felt eerily alone, but there was no turning back at that stage.

By the time I reached the office of the Irish Tourist Board on the corner of Bruton Street, I was truly terrified, but immediately Margaret took me under her wing and assured that I would not be left standing about on my own. True to her word, she introduced me to lots of very interesting people, both Irish and British. After a drinks reception, we moved on to a small West End theatre, where we were treated to the premiere of *Dancing at Lughnasa*.

Following the performance, we retired to a nearby hotel for a sumptuous dinner with lots of wine and further entertainment. Naturally, I spent most of the evening worrying about how I was going to get home to Surrey when the time arrived. It would take more than an hour by train, and I wasn't sure if the service would be regular to my local station at that time of night. I knew that a taxi would cost me £45, but there was no way that I could afford the fare. However, Margaret seemed to sense my plight and without asking arranged for someone to take me home to my door at the end of the evening. My gratitude to her knew no bounds.

Some months later, an envelope arrived with the shamrock on its front. The old recognisable shamrock. It contained an invitation to the Ireland Fund Ball to be held at the Grosvenor Hotel, London. I was absolutely thrilled. The invitation had read 'Marguerite and partner'. Partner. Well, now that was a problem. I didn't know any men in London. Well, I knew some men at work, but none free to leave their wives and accompany me to the Ball. I was like Cinderella without a Prince Charming.

Then there was the other problem. It was black tie which, of course, for me meant a long dress. I didn't possess a formal evening dress. So once again, the major question: What will I wear? I had noticed a second-hand clothes shop near where I lived, which often had some nice evening dresses in the window to buy or to rent. Rent per night, £80. To buy, nothing under £250. And that was second hand. I despaired.

"Buy yourself something decent, Mum. You deserve it," said my daughter. "You're worth it."

But I just couldn't bring myself to believe her. I headed for Oxford Street in the hope of finding a bargain hidden in one of its stores. The bargains made me look like a whore, or even worse, mutton masquerading as lamb. What was I going to do? I wanted to go to the Ball. I needed to have some sort of a life. I could not exist on just work and childminding alone. I strolled in and out of the designer shops on New Bond Street. Escada, Yves St Laurent, Prada, Gucci – they were all there. Oh, for just once in my life to wear a beautiful ball gown like that. Cinderella, I chided, stop dreaming!

Eventually, I compromised. In one of the big department stores on Oxford Street, I came across a glitzy black party number for £80. Well, £80 to rent for one night was daft, but £80 to buy, that was another matter. Well, maybe I might get a chance to wear it again, I thought. Only one problem. It was not full length. It was almost full. Halfway between knee and ankle. Ballet length, I believe describes it. The last time I had been to a black tie affair in Donegal years earlier, women had been wearing similar lengths, so I took the chance that I would get away with it. I mean, just how upmarket could a London Ball be?

This time out, I had opted to stay overnight in London in a small hotel, which was quite reasonable. The invitation had stated 'Carriages at 2 am', and for once I did not want to be worrying about getting home in the middle of the night. By this stage I was out of pocket by £140, £80 for the dress and £60 for the hotel. But I decided to try and enjoy myself. After all, one night out in a year wouldn't make me a raver.

Margaret had arranged for me to meet her and her party in the bar of the hotel at 7 pm and we would all go in together. However, as luck would have it, my train broke down, I couldn't get a taxi at Victoria, and the traffic was bedlam. I arrived at 7.30 pm and naturally they had already gone into the banqueting room. I was terrified and ready to bolt. How would I possibly find her in this throng? As I mingled through the assembled groups, all appearing to know each other, I noticed some extremely stylish outfits on the ladies. Many of the men wore white dinner jackets. I began to feel slightly underdressed. After fifteen minutes of wandering with a bright smile etched across my face, I was rescued by Margaret who had spotted me from afar and made her way towards me. Relief.

She looked superb in a spectacular gold number. Without too much ado, we took our seats at dinner, and I felt safe that I had an allocated place to cling to for safety. Dinner was a most enjoyable and lively affair. However, I did notice that many ladies passing our table were all wearing full-length ball gowns. Too late I realised, that it was not just a long dress affair, it was a total ball gown affair. To be fair, Margaret had mentioned that it would be quite a dressy and fashionable gathering, but I had never anticipated such formality. I sneaked out to the ladies once or twice during the meal, each time trying to pull my dress further down around my ankles.

After dinner, to my horror, the band began to play and it was all hands onto the dance floor. Despite my protestations of tiredness, sore legs, sore back and so on, I was obliged to accompany each of the six males at our table, on a round of the floor.

Please let the floor swallow me up, I pleaded with God. Have you ever tried to dance with your knees permanently bent? I was trying to make the dress look longer, to bring the hem nearer to the floor. But I felt cheap. I felt embarrassed. I felt humiliated. I felt I wanted to cry. I felt rage. Why had my husband landed me in this rotten situation? Why was I stuck there in an anonymous city, at an expensive bash that I could not afford to be at, and on my own in the middle of hundreds of total strangers? Even the beautiful wine could not wipe out my misery. Eventually, my purgatory came to an end and it was time to go home. I grabbed my coat from the cloakroom and attempted to cover myself with it. But even that was futile. All around me ladies were collecting their long fur coats to shield them from the cold night.

As I headed off to hail a taxi, totally on my own, I felt very much like giving up. Back at my hotel, I lay on the bed in my tiny single room high in the loft, and cried. Why was life so horrible? Why did every experience have to turn out to be such a disaster?

13

'The McDaid Affair'

One day in 1991, something very strange, wonderful and heartbreaking happened. The phone rang by my bed. It was my husband, ringing from Dublin.

"I've just left the Boss's office," he said in a hushed conspiratorial tone. "I'm in. He's bringing me in right at the top. Straight into Defence. For God's sake, don't tell anyone."

It was 10 pm at the end of a cold winter's day in Donegal, and I was having another early night. Two years previously, our little family had become fragmented. Husband commuting to and from Dublin every week, daughter at university in London, son at college in Shannon, another son at boarding school in Co Galway, and no one left at home but myself and our little two-year-old. So I had taken to going to bed early to avoid the boredom of the long nights and had just turned out my bedside light when the phone rang.

"Whatever you do, don't tell anyone," he repeated. Well, how *could* I possibly tell anyone? I didn't have a clue what he was talking about.

"James. Slow down a sec. What are you saying?"

"It's Haughey. He's putting me in right at the top."

"The top of what?" I asked.

"Into the Cabinet. Minister for Defence," he said.

"Do you mean Junior Minister?" I queried. The newspapers earlier in the week had mentioned his name as an outside possibility for a junior post but we were ignoring all that. No point in raising hopes only to have them dashed, he had said.

"No. Full Cabinet Minister. Minister for Defence. Christ, I'm shaking like a leaf," he continued. "Christ, whatever you do, don't tell a soul. It can't get out until tomorrow. It'll all be announced on the 11 o'clock news tomorrow morning."

There was silence at my end. Stunned silence. He had told me many tall tales in his lifetime, but this was a big one. Had he hit the juice in a big way? Was he going mad? Worse still, had *I* already gone mad?

"My God. Are you sure that's what he said?" I asked again.

It seemed like only yesterday that the word 'politics' had first entered our lives. Now all of a sudden, two years later, and with no prior warning, he was being catapulted into one of the highest offices in the State. Then both of us started to laugh.

"Jesus Christ, James, this is unbelievable. Now I'm shaking," I said, genuinely excited. "This is just brilliant. I wish I was in Dublin with you."

"I know. I don't know how I'm going to get a wink of sleep tonight."

After a lot more banter, he rang off, saying he would ring me first thing in the morning when he had more information.

"But for God's sake, don't tell anyone."

I lay back on the pillow and the tears began. Tears of absolute joy and happiness, and tears of disbelief. Five minutes later, I jumped out of bed and ran up and down the long hallway of our bungalow talking to myself. I needed to thank God out loud. Was this God's way of making up for the previous troubled years? Was this the break we had been waiting for, the break our family needed? Somewhere in the middle of the night I found sleep.

The next day, Wednesday, 13 November 1991 dawned bright, and I woke unsure if I had dreamt the events of the previous night. In the bedroom next door, a little voice was calling to be lifted from his cot. I scooped him up in my arms, never more grateful for a human body to hug. The phone rang. It was James.

"I'm in the Dáil now and it's all going ahead. I'm up to my neck in it, being briefed for the job and for interviews, so I have to dash," he said. "Get yourself organised to come to Dublin as soon as you can after the announcement on TV. Book a couple of rooms in Jury's Hotel before you leave. And you better ring your mother now and warn her, in case she has a heart attack when she sees the TV. I'll see you in a few hours. Love you." And he was gone.

Little did I realise that this was the last jollity I would hear in his voice for months to come.

"We now go over live to Leinster House for a special news bulletin," said the RTÉ announcer. Every bone in my body was trembling and the toddler had chosen that moment to empty the contents of the kitchen cupboards onto the floor. But I didn't care. Then I saw him standing on the plinth, flanked by 'The Boss' and his close friend and colleague, Noel Davern from Tipperary. The pride I had felt in him at the local count centre on the night of his election to the Dáil two years earlier was nothing compared to this. My eyes filled with tears and I wanted to hug the television. I had never seen him look so radiant and so happy.

Five minutes later, our driveway was filled with cars, the phone was hopping and the house crammed with friends and well-wishers. Grown men were leaping and dancing around the kitchen, hugging each other with glee. I had never before seen anything like it. I was trying in vain to get in touch with my children, but the phone just kept on ringing, each time I replaced the receiver. No mobile phones unfortunately in 1991! Two hours later, I was on the road to Dublin in my car. I needed to make the journey alone, to sort my head out. But first, James had instructed me to go to the local bank and withdraw some cash. It was going to be one hell of a celebration in Dublin. The bank manager that day jokingly asked me, if I would like to borrow £100,000!

This was my first realisation that there would be an increase in salary. For years, we had been broke and up to our eyes in debt. I was tired of always scrimping and saving. Was this to be the end of our financial troubles? Hopefully. On the road out of town, I stopped to let a friend cross the road. He was bundled up in a warm woolly hat and overcoat, and looked frozen in the warm wintry sunshine. His face was pale and gaunt as he saluted me. He doesn't look his usually healthy and bouncy self, I had thought to myself. He probably has the flu. Three months later, he died from lung cancer. Every time I think of that day, his face is the first thing that comes to my mind.

In the car, I relaxed and basked in pleasurable thoughts. I contemplated how this would change our lives. How lucky we were. The Fianna Fáilers in the house that morning had mentioned a ten-foot wall being built around our house, with armed Gardaí in a hut in the garden. I smiled at the ridiculousness of the idea.

"You'll be driven everywhere in a Merc by a chauffeur," they said.

What an odd experience that would be.

"You'll have to move to Dublin," they added. That was not a bad option, I thought. But the most important factor in my own mind was in no way related to any of the above. For so many years of our marriage, alcohol had reared its ugly head in our family life. Now, under the scrutiny of media publicity, and the high profile of the job in question, one could not afford to be seen on the wrong side of a bottle of Hennessy. Peace, tranquillity and sobriety, I believed, were about to take over our lives. No more hurt, no more worrying, no more waiting.

Monaghan is the halfway point between Donegal and Dublin, and as I drove through the main street I toyed with the idea of stopping to buy myself something new to wear. But old habits are hard to break and thrift got the better of me. I was still unable to spend money on myself, even with the prospect of a huge rise in salary. Then it was on to Castleblaney where I stopped for a cup of tea in a local hotel. It was 5 pm. The TV in the bar was showing the news headlines, and there he was on the screen, still standing on the plinth. I could not actually hear what was being said, but I was not worried, as I presumed he had spent most of the day giving interviews. Then some PDs and Fine Gaelers appeared, but I paid little heed to them. I just wanted to get to Dublin as quickly as possible. I wanted to see him in the flesh and not on a screen. I wanted to hug him and tell him how proud I was of him.

Leinster House was ablaze with lights at 7 pm when I drove up to the gates. There were TV cameras, photographers and reporters everywhere. The security officials on the gate recognised me and waved my car into a parking space with radiant smiles on their faces.

"Congratulations, Mrs McDaid," they called through the open window. I felt extremely privileged. Next through the huge revolving doors into the foyer, where the ushers called out their congratulations.

"I think he's in the private bar," one called. "I'll take you there and call him for you." Everyone was being really nice and I was being treated like royalty. I felt tremendously honoured. In the Members' Bar, as I waited for him, his colleagues came and shook hands, offered congratulations and assured me that everything would be okay.

"Don't worry," they said.

Worry about what, I thought fleetingly. Then the 'Father of the House', Neil Blaney, approached me and asked me to join him for a drink. This took me slightly by surprise, as rivalry between FF and Independent FF was at its strongest in Donegal North East at that time. I had barely taken a sip of my drink when Michael Woods approached me and asked me to go with him to my husband's office. I would have preferred to wait for him in the bar, but he explained that James was busy at a meeting with Mr Haughey. Outside the Members' Bar, I was handed over to another colleague who escorted me along a back corridor to my husband's office.

There I was left in the capable hands of an official from the Department of Defence. I still had no inkling of what was taking place somewhere in the bowels of Leinster House. The TV monitor in my husband's office showed the Dáil chamber beginning to fill up as the deputies took their seats.

"I'm afraid there have been some objections to Jim's appointment," said the official at my side, his face taking on a painful grimace.

"How do you mean?" I asked, still suspecting nothing.

"Well, they may be able to get round it. I don't know yet," he said in worried tones.

"The PDs are objecting to the appointment. Something to do with an old photograph that Fine Gael has thrown up."

Then the phone rang and he answered it. "Yes. Yes. Okay. Yes. Okay," was all I heard before he replaced the receiver.

"Jim is coming into the chamber now," he told me.

I watched the monitor and caught a glimpse of my husband as he took his seat. But his face was set in a tight grimace. Why was he not smiling? Was something wrong? Then a deafening hush set over the chamber as he rose to his feet and the camera focused on him alone. He looked like death. My heart was thumping.

"In view of the attacks…and in the broader national interest…I have requested the Taoiseach to withdraw my nomination as a member of the Government."

My mind screamed, what is he saying? What is he talking about? Stop saying that, James. The room was swimming around me. And then it was all over. Just as suddenly as it had all begun, it had finished. It was like watching something one loved slip down a stream, out of reach, out of sight around the bend in the river. Gone beyond rescue. An innocent photograph of my husband taken beside a constituent, Jim Clarke – a Republican – on his release from prison some years earlier, had brought his ministerial role to an end, after just eight hours. I sat at his desk, numb, unsure even of what had happened. The sympathetic official offered words of comfort and then beat a relieved retreat. My God, what *had* happened?

One hour earlier I had been waiting with bated breath to throw my arms around him and celebrate his and my good fortune. But I never got the chance. Before I could even touch him, everything was gone.

I had watched the monitor as the man, who earlier that day had bounced before the cameras, suddenly transformed into a tortured soul before my eyes. I needed to find him. I needed to be with him. I needed to hug him and tell him everything would be all right. But it was two hours before I was given that chance. In the meantime, I sat at his desk, answering his phone as it rang with hundreds of messages of support. The men who had earlier that day danced in my kitchen in Donegal, now literally wept over the phone to me.

Eventually, a colleague of my husband's came and took me back to the Members' Bar. I had been unsure what to do or where to go after the 'bomb' had exploded. As I entered the bar, people came from everywhere to shake my hand and to sympathise – men and women from all parties. Drinks were being pressed into my hand but I had no desire for them. When James walked in fifteen minutes later, the rousing cheer that greeted him was overwhelming and extremely heart-warming. It brought both of us to the brink of tears. We hugged each other, but words were not appropriate. I could feel his pain like a knife in my own body.

The remainder of that evening passed in a blurred wave of condolence and support. Around the circular bar in Jury's Hotel, fellow politicians expressed their feelings of disbelief and disgust. Fellow TDs from all parties were of the same sentiments, even if they did not express them as openly as on that night in Jury's. Friends and family rallied round. Somewhere in the small hours we sought an exhausted and fitful sleep in one of Jury's premier rooms.

It was 7 am the next morning and somewhere in my head a phone was ringing.

"Good morning, Mrs McDaid. This is RTÉ. Is it possible to speak to Dr McDaid please?"

I looked at the sleeping figure in the bed beside me and asked them nicely to call back in an hour. I explained that he needed some more sleep and they understood. After what he had been through, he deserved some rest. The nightmare of yesterday was hammering in my head. I was having difficulty blotting it out. I just wanted us to get back to Donegal and put this nightmare behind us. Above all, I really needed to contact my children. Worst of all, that day was my only daughter's twenty-first birthday. She was at college in London and I had spent the previous week making sure that all her gifts and flowers would arrive at precisely 11 am that day.

I dressed quietly and went to get a newspaper to see if there was anything written about the events of the previous day. Probably not very much, I thought. As I reached the newspaper stand outside Jury's, my head began to swim. Up to this point in my life, the only publicity attached to our family was some small photos in the local papers following the General Election two years earlier. Now as I looked down I saw my own face staring back at me from the front page of every national title on the stand: *The Irish Times, Irish Independent, Irish Press, Irish Mirror.* All of them.

Somehow it had not registered the previous evening as dozens of cameras snapped that he and I would actually appear on the front page. The photographs were so large that it felt like I was jumping out at myself. That moment, in particular, stands out as one of the strangest sensations in my life. It is still very difficult to explain how it felt to know that thousands of people that morning were looking at us over their toast and cornflakes. It felt quite disturbing and somewhat intrusive. Little did I realise then, that in years to come, many less pleasant images of my family would dominate the front pages. I bought a copy of each title and carried them back to our hotel room. I noticed some early risers looking at me, and wondered why. Was my hair standing on the top of my head, or had I grown an extra nose? Back in the privacy of the bedroom, I started to investigate further. My God. I was in shock.

Not only did the front pages carry the story, but inside there were also pages and pages of photographs and opinions. I had never seen anything like it. At 8 am I woke my husband and he went live on RTÉ, as promised. It was a strange morning. He did not want to speak to me about it.

He wanted to go back to Leinster House and continue as usual. I don't think that even he anticipated the fallout that would continue for days to come. Later that day, we sat lethargically in the back of a taxi, going through Rathmines on the way to RTÉ. He had been asked to do a news programme that night. I felt a great emotional pain inside me. I was finding it difficult to breath effectively.

"This is like having an operation without any anaesthetic," I said to him.

I could feel his pain as well as my own. He was silent and introspective and hurting badly, that I knew. I felt I should be able to fix the situation for him, somehow. But I couldn't.

The entire fiasco was difficult to describe. Perhaps like being told that you have won the lottery, only to find out a few hours later that the ticket was invalid. Something like that. It was not a prize that we had asked for or expected, but its coming had brought positive feelings and happiness to a lot of people. I had eventually managed to get in touch with my daughter to explain what had happened. Now she was distraught for her father, and any form of celebration of her twenty-first immediately went up in smoke. My heart went out to her. Another big day in her life ruined.

The events of the 13 November 1991 have been recorded in many publications since then as 'The Mc Daid Affair'. The outcome of those events resulted in his overwhelming, all-consuming hunger for power. Having tasted at the table of high office, even for only eight hours, the determination was set to regain that position of power. No effort would be spared in the pursuit of that goal. A tough impermeable protective barricade was erected, leaving a body of stone. Sadly, when that goal was achieved six years later, the warmth and the smiles had long disappeared, leaving only the shell of my husband.

14

Christmas 1998

Our first Christmas away from our home, away from all the family. Some people love Christmas and some hate it. I belong to the first group. My love of the event stems from my childhood and from my father. Year after year, he turned it into a truly magical event. This was not because of lavish expensive presents or extravagant entertaining. Each year there was the just one gift from Santa, which would not have been excessive. In addition to this, he would hide other little gifts around the living room and then tease us with clues as to where to look. I remember finding a tiny doll the size of my thumb, hidden behind the couch when I was about six. I treasured it for years. When my father was six-years-old, his mother died on Christmas Eve, close to her twenty-eighth birthday. She was an unfortunate victim of that terrible flu epidemic that plagued Europe around 1918. He used to tell us that his abiding memory of Christmas morning was of seeing his mother in her coffin. I think that is why he went to so much trouble to make Christmas such a special time for us children, and also for himself. I can still picture him tucking me up in bed the week before the big day, and telling me wonderful Christmas stories that he would conjure up from old local folktales of Co Longford, where he grew up.

It was from him that I formed my basic values in life. For me, my children, love and friendship are the important things. Not lots of money or power, or what other people think of us. Throughout my own children's formative years, I made every effort to keep that magic alive, although my father had unfortunately died shortly after our first child was born. By then, the season of mirth and joyfulness contained a lot more clinking of glasses and opening of bottles, accompanied by the necessity to go to the pub on Christmas Eve. Not the best recipe for peace and tranquillity. I don't know if I succeeded with my own children as well as my father did, but I believe that some of them still hold on to that magic.

Christmas 1998 would be so entirely different from all those others. Strangely enough, for the first time in quite a few years, I actually looked forward to it. I knew it would be so different, and possibly very lonely, but I also knew that it would be very peaceful.

I started to think back to Christmases in Donegal over the previous years. Due to my husband's popularity and generosity as a local GP, his patients repaid him with Christmas gifts too numerous to mention. There were enough turkeys to start our own farm, joints of ham and sides of smoked salmon, and enough Christmas cakes to feed us through to the following year and beyond. There were enough bottles of spirits to refloat the *Titanic* and enough aftershave to keep him smelling of roses for life. One of the gifts I appreciated most one year was a surprise giant basket of vegetables and fruit. It contained everything conceivable, from sprouts to satsumas, mushrooms to mangoes. There were also gifts of books, clothes, pens, lamps, jewellery, pictures, ornaments and anything else you can imagine. One Christmas Eve, I counted over seventy packages for him to open the next morning. When the children were younger, we all got great fun from helping him open his gifts. It was certainly one of the things we would all miss that Christmas.

Another thing I would miss was Mass on Christmas morning. I am not religious in that sense, but I always loved the feeling of warmth and goodwill, and seeing my friends and neighbours singing their hearts out. I loved the way everyone joined in with *Hark the Herald Angels Sing* at the end of Mass, because everyone knew the words. Christmas in a strange church in London would not, I felt, be the same.

Cooking Christmas dinner was another treat I always enjoyed. I never looked on it as a chore. Some people love to get it over with and out of the way as early as possible, but to us, it was the highlight of the day. I loved to do it all exactly as my mother had done for years, which was all very traditional. Indeed, no one could equal her recipe for turkey gravy with giblets.

Another great enjoyment was playing tennis on St Stephen's Day. This was something I had begun to organise a few years earlier, where sixteen of us got together in the afternoon and played a very friendly mixed tournament. It was a great way to work off the excesses of the previous day for the adults, and for the children it was an excuse to drag them away from their computer games. My older sons and my son-in-law also joined in. Then, after all that exercise, it was back to a party in our house for the night, to quench our thirst.

So now my son was beginning the build-up to Christmas '98 and I was trying my level best to summon some enthusiasm. I smiled a lot and played a great game of pretence when he listed out what presents everyone would be getting and what we would be doing for the big day. He plagued me daily to visit the garden centre and get a tree.

"No, we can't get a fake one, Mum," he begged. "We never have a fake one. You can't smell anything from a fake one."

We compromised in the garden centre and purchased a type of midget tree. Our flat was too tiny to house a lifesized version. But he didn't mind as long as it was real. I joined him in the decorating two weeks before the 25th and he was happy. I was just beginning to get on top of the situation and quite looking forward to Christmas when another one of those trains came hurtling out of the tunnel and hit me full on in the face. It came in a brown envelope on the 17th December. I knew even before I opened the envelope that it was 'legal'. You always know by those strong envelopes they use.

> *Dear Mrs McDaid,*
>
> *We have been instructed, etc., etc.,…husband…requires…legal separation….*
>
> *Yours etc.,…*

Brief and to the point. Cutting, hurtful and insensitive. And so perfectly timed. Just a week to go to Christmas. It hit me and knocked me flat. Now I had to keep a brave face on it for Luke, if I could. But then, my husband's timing was simply par for the course. His *modus operandi* did not pay heed to feelings.

But heck, this was London, I thought. Surely we could lose our troubles in the big city. Once the lights went up in Oxford Street and Regent Street, London took on a really festive feeling. Even the thousands of commuters attempted a smile on the train in the mornings. In early December I had taken my son and his friend to Oxford Street to see the switching on of the lights. That year, a little bit of Ireland was present in the form of Ronan Keating, who performed the opening ceremony. So now to cheer us up, I took my son and grandson Cameron to see the shop window displays in Selfridges and Hamleys. The former was nine and probably considered himself a little bit too old, and possibly a bit too 'cool' for the magic of the displays, but I watched with great pleasure as Cameron tried to take in what it all meant.

My own personal favourite Christmas shopping trip was to the King's Road in Chelsea and the area around Sloane Square. During the late sixties, when I had worked in London, the King's Road was in its prime. Today, it still retains some of that magic. One often sees ageing rockers strolling along, as though trapped in a time warp. On the other hand, there is a definite air of elegance about it. It is a great street for 'just looking'. One Saturday morning, we shook hands with Jeffrey Archer outside Chelsea Town Hall, as he canvassed in his bid to become Mayor of London. The following Saturday, he had fallen to the ground like a rotting apple. Such is politics. How easily the mighty tumble! The other end of the King's Road – the World's End area – is dotted with little Italian cafés, some of which have been there for years and are still selling great food at practically seventies prices.

Back in our flat in Surrey, we wrapped lots of small presents and put them under the tree, a week before Christmas. For me, it's not the price tag that matters. Indeed the monetary value is far removed from my idea of what Christmas should mean. I believe that Christmas should be about choosing a small gift, price irrelevant, which is really a token way of saying, 'I have thought about you and this is what I would like you to have, and when you see it you will think of me.'

Every night my son would count the packages and rearrange them. We would then talk about presents given and received in previous years. One Christmas, I gave the love of my life an iron. Yes, a simple shiny new domestic iron, with steam control, of course. On Christmas morning, the family looked aghast as he unwrapped his gift, until I explained my choice to them all. You see in recent years, my husband had become paranoid about his appearance, and in particular his white shirts. He had reached the point where I was not allowed to wash or iron them, as I did not get them white enough to match his sparkling teeth. A long process of soaking and sterilising would take place each week (his shirts, not his teeth!). To this end, he employed the services of Napisan. If you are old enough and produced babies in the seventies as I did, then you will remember that your hands spent a large portion of the day immersed in the stuff, as you struggled to sterilise your baby's towelling or cloth nappies. Somewhere in Dublin, James had been given this gem of household science, and became relentless in his pursuit of perfect whiteness. A large bucket was employed for this operation, and each week on his return from Dublin, his white shirts were his main priority. Straightaway they were put into the magic mixture. It was necessary to keep this bucket in the living area, so that he could keep an eye on it at all times. Many attempts by me to remove it to less conspicuous quarters were met with antagonism. At regular intervals throughout the weekend, the bucket would be bent over and its contents moved about and checked for any possible areas not fully submerged. On one unfortunate occasion, as he was bent laboriously over his chore, there was a loud splash followed by an even louder verbal obscenity. Sadly, his mobile phone, which was permanently attached to his ear, had slipped silently from his breast pocket and taken a deep dive into the bucket of Napisan. Now that would surely clean up the ministerial mobile. It was unfortunate that most of the family was in the room at the time, and we found it very difficult to restrain our giggles. For some strange reason, he failed to see the funnier side. But then, he failed to find humour in most things. Life was to be endured, not enjoyed.

But getting back to the shirts. One warm sunny day, I inadvertently took five shirts from the washing machine and hung them out on the clothes line to dry, as you do. Seeking praise and validation, I suppose. One hour later, he arrived home and my crime was discovered.

"Never hang my shirts in the sunshine," he bellowed. "It makes them go yellow. Never put them out on the line again."

Ah well, I cannot do anything right. I know. Instead, the shirts were draped over the backs of chairs throughout the house and the central heating turned up. Everywhere one looked there was a wet shirt. It was like living in a laundry. Once steeped, washed and dried under strictly controlled conditions, he would then struggle to bring his prized collection to a final pristine crispness with an ancient and faulty iron, blighted by limescale and scorch marks. So when I presented him with his very own state-of-the-art model, he was chuffed. Now that is what I call putting thought into a gift.

It must have been some time after this, that I figured it might be time to broach the subject of a tumble dryer with him. The weather had been dreadful for months and I was tired of wet washing sitting on radiators. Well, I figured that after twenty-seven years of marriage, it was time I started thinking about some labour-saving devices. My daughter had a tumble dryer, my son had a tumble dryer, my friends had tumble dryers, so why not me? So I prepared what I would say, and put the proposition to him one day when he appeared to be in a good mood. It had been pouring rain for four days, with no sign of any let up.

"Maybe we should get a tumble dryer," I ventured hesitantly.

But, I should have known better.

"You must be joking," came the reply. "Where do you think I am going to get the money for that? There's no need for one. There are plenty of radiators to dry clothes on. There's no space to put in the kitchen…" And so on and so forth.

"We could put it in one of the spare bedrooms," I suggested. We did not have a utility room or garage in the house.

"Now you want to go ruining the bedrooms. Can you not just leave the house alone for once instead of always trying to ruin it? Is it any wonder we never have any money, when you keep coming up with all these hair-brained ideas? There will be no tumble dryer and that is final."

End of story. But in a sarcastic moment, I bravely ventured, "Well, if you give me the money for a good hairdryer with a strong motor, then I could stand out at the line and blow-dry the clothes, I suppose."

Again I thought, I am a terrible person. I should not be upsetting him like this. I am bad. I am selfish. But I thought £120 was not really that much to ask for. I had even suggested that we could get it on hire purchase, paying it off each month. But he wasn't having any of it.

Two months later, I was in the local electrical shop again and it was still raining. On an impulse, I decided I had enough of wet clothes.

"I've decided to go for the tumble dryer after all," I told the salesman.

He knew I had been toying with the idea for months.

"Great. We'll deliver it to you tomorrow," he said.

"Oh no," I almost jumped with fright.

Tomorrow would be Friday and the boss would be back from Dublin.

"You'll have to leave it until next Tuesday. I'll ring you when he's gone back to Dublin and it will be safe to bring it in then."

I signed up for the hire purchase agreement and decided to pay for it out of my children's allowance each month. It was the cheapest model in the shop but as long as it did the job, I didn't care.

Tuesday morning James left for Dublin early, and my plan went into action. I rang the shop and one hour later, the *pièce de résistance* arrived. I was like an excited child. The delivery men were quite amused that I should choose to place a tumble dryer in our own bedroom.

"Are you sure you don't want it someplace else?" their eyes told me. Right crackpot here, they figured.

Pushed well into the corner, covered with a heavy tablecloth, vase of flowers and some photographs of the children atop, we had a nice display unit. And there it remained hidden, except between Tuesday and Thursday each week, when it would spurt into action. What joy! All the weekly laundry completed in two days. Of course even at that, I still would not put clothes straight from the washing machine into the dryer. Instead I would get as much moisture out as possible through various methods. I was terrified that he would spot any increase in the ESB bill.

If I needed to use the dryer at weekends, I would wait until he went out and then position my young son at the bedroom window, where he was trained to shout to me downstairs if he spotted his father's car coming up the road. Once we were almost caught out when Luke's little friend walking past the house distracted his attention. But my lightening reaction detained him downstairs until the heat in the bedroom had dissipated.

For six months we played our game of deception. James slept in that room, dressed in it and walked around it, yet never spotted the object in the corner. Then one day, he arrived back unexpectedly from Dublin. I was caught with my guard down. The tablecloth was recklessly thrown back and the forbidden fruit was naked. Well, it was only Wednesday and I was in 'relax' mode.

"Where did that come from?" he demanded. "I thought we agreed there would be no tumble dryer."

"How much did that cost me?" he roared.

"Actually, it has already been paid for," I lied. The final payment was in fact due in two months.

"Once again, you ignore my advice," he barked and stormed out of the house.

As it turned out, the tumble dryer stayed. Having finally recognised its benefits, he would fill it with socks and boxer shorts. Needless to say, the shirts still took pride of place on the radiators.

But back to Christmas presents. Two years ago I bought James a book. Not just any old book, but the long-running bestseller, *Men are from Mars, Women are from Venus.* I had been given a copy by a workmate some months earlier and found it fascinating. Among its many interesting ideas on the difference between the sexes, was the one on men and their caves. The author's theory goes something like this: When men are feeling down or fed up about something, they will by their very nature, retreat into what is called their 'cave'. Here they want to be left alone, for an unspecified time, to work things out by themselves. Then hopefully, they will emerge, refreshed and willing to communicate with their partner. Women, however, in a similar frame of mind, will seek comfort and a sympathetic and supportive ear from their other half. They don't go into caves. This is where it all gets so complicated. Men assume, mistakenly, that women want to be left alone, as they themselves do, and women think that men want to be comforted, just as they would wish their partner to comfort them.

"Why can we not talk about it?" the women wail from the rooftops. Aha. This is the big mistake. Women follow men into their caves and try to drag them out to 'talk about it'.

Men dig themselves in deeper inside their caves. Was this what I had been doing wrong? Following him into his cave and trying to sort out his problems for him. Maybe I had.

So I gave him the book, complete with a written apology for years of not understanding that I did not need to go into his cave to make him happy. On the other hand, I recognised that I had needed him to support and comfort me when I was feeling down, but he had not known this either. What a pity that book had not been printed twenty years earlier. One of my sons reacted to such 'pop psychology' with a good hearty laugh. But my husband, suspicious of my motives, left the book aside. Ever the politician when faced with the unknown, he had no comment to make.

In the run-up to the big day in 1998, my daughter would often chide me with a warning.

"Now Mum, no furry hot-water bottles this Christmas, please."

She was referring back to when she was fourteen and rebellious. It is that time in a teenager's life when they do not need to wear warm clothes (they think), and instead spend the winter shivering in skimpy tops. We've all done it, because it is 'cool'. Well, I thought, she could at least be warm in bed at night when none of her friends are watching, so I bought her a fluffy bright pink hot-water bottle. This contrasted perfectly with her entirely black gothic wardrobe at the time, but for some odd reason, she was not amused or excited by my choice of gift. As she matured, however, she came to understand the love behind the gift and would probably do the same now for her own children.

We sent lots of cards from London, more than we had ever sent when we lived in Ireland. I hoped that we would get plenty back, to add to Luke's excitement. Thankfully, we did. There is nothing like being far away from one's friends and family for a long time to make one appreciate the postman. It was extremely difficult to summon up the enthusiasm for all of this, but I wanted to make up to Luke for all the trauma of having to leave his home, move to a new school and make new friends. We went shopping and bought loads of food, most of which I knew we could never eat between the two of us. But it was nice to have that feeling of a well-stocked larder, just in case! A bit of traditional stocking up in case of floods or famine, naturally! And true to form I stockpiled lots of tins of sliced peaches and packets of cheesy crackers.

One of the things I had particularly looked forward to that year was taking part in a major performance of Handel's *Messiah* with a group of choirs, accompanied by a full symphony orchestra from Surrey. An extra bonus was that my son would also be on stage with me as part of his school's chapel choir. It would have been a memorable event for both of us, and something I had wanted to do for years, but unfortunately after weeks of practice, I was forced to drop out. Rushing home from work in London to Surrey for rehearsals two nights a week had begun to take its toll, and eventually added just more stress to my life. However, I did attend the performance and the sound they produced was truly magnificent, the type of thing that makes the hairs stand on the back of one's neck.

I felt so proud of my son. It was at times like this that my spirits rose, and I was glad that I had brought him to London to be part of something special like that event. It almost made it all worthwhile. As it turned out, we had a very nice Christmas. Different, but nice. Peaceful. No worries about people being in bad form and affecting everyone else in the house. My daughter had invited us to spend Christmas with her and her family, and along with one of my older sons, who had come over from Ireland, we had a good day. The most important thing was my young son went to bed that night, happy and content. That was all that mattered.

15

Platform 12

I have always loved the company of men. Having had no brothers
in my family, I find them fascinating, as I did my father who was an
extremely open and affectionate man. He was my role model,
dedicated to his home and to his children. Marriage then, in my book,
meant two people making a commitment to each other to share their
lives together. This should not mean living exclusively in each other's
pockets, but living side-by-side and coming together on a regular basis
to share their companionship, their joys, their children, their sadness,
their hopes, their worries, and their love.

Being in a marriage on one's own is a very lonely place to be. Like the
sound of one hand clapping, perhaps. Empty. Silent. One partner has
so much to give, but the other unwilling to receive. Thus I saw my life.
Family life, marriage, trust and fidelity were of no value it seemed. I had
lots of very good friends and managed to rekindle a fairly decent social
life once my children were that little bit older and no longer required
me for their every need.

Yet I longed for my husband's company, but sadly he was unwilling
to socialise with me or with any of our friends. He did not like going
out with other couples. He did not like going out to dinner. He did not
like visiting friends' houses. He was unwilling to entertain at home,
even though I was an enthusiastic cook. I loved cooking for dinner
parties, but he was having none of it. His idea of a night out was
standing against the bar of his local, chatting to the lads about football
and horses. And there's nothing wrong with that, now and again. Even

though it seems to be the prerogative of the Irish male. But when it precludes all other forms of socialising, then it begins to wear a bit thin.

It may seem strange, but I just longed for something very simple. I longed to just sit down with my husband over a bottle of wine and enjoy each other's company. Just once would have sufficed. Like we did when we were first married. But it was out of the question.

Then one evening, when I was in Dublin, I managed to do just that. But the man was not my husband. It was a chance meeting with someone I had known for years. Together we sat and shared a bottle of wine and talked for hours. It was unbelievable. I felt like a weight had been lifted from my shoulders. We talked and we laughed and we smiled. When had I last smiled like that? God knows. I felt perfectly relaxed for the first time in years. The term soulmate can have all sorts of connotations, but this was what I felt with this man. For once, I could speak without being judged or criticised. I could offer an opinion without being told I was stupid. I could sit and drink wine safe in the knowledge that I wouldn't have to stay on drinking till the small hours and then carry my companion home, undress him and put him to bed and then lie awake listening to him snoring beside me. This companionship had no hidden agenda. And so developed one of the greatest friendships I was ever to forge in my life, and one that remains strong to this day.

Another man that I was to turn to in times of trouble, but also in times of joy, was a friend from my earliest childhood. Again in this case, we happened upon each other one day totally by accident. Once again, we developed a strong friendship, where we shared our worries and woes, and learnt to rely on each other for support in times of crisis. Both of these friendships are very much valued, and but for them I would not have got through many debilitating and terrifying episodes during my married life. Of course, it is extremely difficult to convince onlookers that a friendship between two people of the opposite sex can be platonic. But then that is the risk one must take if a friendship is worth having in the first instance.

During the many years of my husband's reliance on alcohol, a number of his 'friends' assumed that because of his unconcern for his wife, it might be no harm to see how far they might get with this pathetic woman. Sadly, in my desperate and unhappy state, and in a valiant effort to get my husband's attention, I played along with their sick games when I was very low. Rubbing their legs against mine under the hidden depths of the pub table was like a challenge to them, especially with my husband sitting just inches away. I could hear their minds clicking, 'How far would I get with the Doc's wife?'

I dreaded attending dinner dances and functions where I was obliged to dance with these men. Why did so many of his friends feel the need to press their bodies against me? Why did they need to let their hands wander so far down my back? Why did they have to breathe so deeply into my ear? Were they trying to make him notice? They were wasting their time. He was too busy doing the same thing to other women, having one affair after another. They were just following his lead. It was all disgusting and humiliating.

Some were not quite so subtle. On one occasion while staying at a friend's house in Dublin with a number of other couples, one of them climbed into bed with me as I lay down for a rest on a Sunday afternoon, following a particularly boozy lunch. Friends, my hat! I came to and screamed just in the nick of time. He had locked the door from the inside but managed to escape through the bedroom window, which fortunately for him was on the ground floor. My husband and some others heard my screams and came rushing to the room. I managed to open the door but was severely traumatised. In an instant, my husband turned and went back to join the party, leading me to believe that if someone else wanted me, then they could have me. I felt sick at the entire set up. This man's wife was only yards away and this was his idea of friendship. I could not wait to get back home to the safety of my own house.

While in London, I took to imagining what it would be like to have a cherished partner. Then one day while waiting for a train in Victoria

Station, life seemed to hold some promise again. The public address system had crackled to life.

This is an announcement for passengers awaiting the 17.34 service to Caterham. There is a…muffle muffle…crackle crackle…with this service.

I looked around me. All the commuters standing under the noticeboard awaiting the 17.34 looked quizzically at the signs above their heads. I had not understood fully what the announcer had said. I looked to my right and saw a white-haired man that I had noticed travelling on that train for the last few weeks. After some hesitation, I decided to ask him what the announcement had said.

"Excuse me," I started falteringly, "Do you know what that said?"

The man turned slightly towards me.

"I have no idea," he replied. "I think it was something about a platform change."

"Oh, thank you," I replied.

I considered saying something else to him, but decided against it, as I did not want to be seen as a nuisance. Anyway, I figured, if he had been interested in talking to me, he would have continued the conversation.

Five minutes later, the platform number appeared on the board above our heads. Platform 12, just like every other day. I set off down the platform as the train approached. Each evening I went to the same carriage. The white-haired stranger also went to that same carriage. As I stood by the door of the train, waiting for it to open, I noticed that he was standing nearby. What a pity he did not speak back to me, I thought. He looked quite nice. But he was probably just another happily married man. I got into the carriage and decided that even though he was not going to speak, at least I could sit and observe him. It would help pass some of the journey instead of reading my *Evening Standard*. I sat across the aisle from him, facing him so that I could observe him without him noticing. He had his head buried in his copy of the *Evening Standard*, but looked up occasionally when people passed by. Unfortunately, however, he never looked in my direction.

Some weeks later, I found myself looking at this stranger again. This time, he sat directly opposite me. I was now able to observe everything about him close up. Starting at his shoes. Yes, they were clean and shining and not worn down at the heels. Next his socks. Yes, nice dark grey, to match his suit. Good so far. Now his trousers. Very nice crease down the front. Always a good sign. So far, everything pointed towards a well-groomed man. His shirt and tie were very positive. A nice blue shirt, well ironed, and a nice tie with a dash of colour. Next I noticed his hands. They were slim and smooth. Not rough like some men's hands. His nails were perfectly groomed and spotlessly clean. Another good sign. Then came the crowning glory. His hair. It was the most beautiful white hair, not a dirty grey like some men, but silky white. And to add to this, his face was partly covered in the same lovely white beard. He looked very distinguished, indeed. But the nicest thing of all was still to come. When he removed his glasses, underneath were hidden two dazzling dark-blue eyes. They were very serious eyes, but I could just imagine how they would look if they were smiling.

Still he kept reading his newspaper. I wondered what he was reading, or what parts of the paper he found interesting. I had my own copy of the *Standard*, so I opened it at the page that he appeared to be reading. He was at the letters page, so that did not tell me very much. At one stage, as I was uncrossing my legs, I almost kicked him on the shin by accident, brushing my toe off his trouser leg, but he didn't seem to notice.

When we both got off the train, I watched him go down the steps from the station and wondered if he was going home to eat his M&S microwave meal for one, or if he had a wife and children at home waiting for him. Ah well, I would probably never be able to answer that question. At the bottom of the steps, I turned left into the darkness, and he turned right, to some unknown destination.

Some weeks later the noticeboard for Caterham had something written underneath in red writing. I strained my eyes to see what it said. But I couldn't make it out. Three months earlier, I had lost my glasses in the newsagents at the station, and was unable to afford a replacement pair. I glanced around and saw the white-haired stranger standing close by. I was unsure if I should interrupt his thoughts again, slightly afraid that he might tell me to leave him alone. From my time in London I had gathered that commuters did not speak to each other. However, I could not read the message, so I got my courage together and addressed him again.

"Excuse me," I began. "Can you tell me what it says on the sign for Caterham?"

"It says the train has been delayed," he said.

This time he smiled slightly as he spoke, and I caught a glimpse of the bright smiling eyes that I had observed some weeks earlier.

"Thank you," I replied.

He nodded as if to say, 'you're welcome', but then spoke no more.

The previous week, I had spent some time looking at properties to buy in the Sandersted area close to where I was now renting a flat. Sandersted was the direction in which this man headed every evening when he left the station. I decided it would be quite reasonable to ask his advice on what the area was like, so I braved it once more.

"Excuse me," I began. "I noticed that when you get off the train you head in the Sandersted direction. I've been looking at a property to buy there, and I was wondering what the area was like, or if you would recommend it?"

"Yes, it's very nice," he replied. "Yes, I would recommend it. Definitely. Where exactly was the property you saw?"

And so we continued to talk until the sign came up for Platform 12. And then we walked along the platform together. I was unsure if I should have thanked him for the information and left him to get on with his journey and his evening paper. But just as we were about to board the train he asked me a question.

"What brings you to England then?"

"Eh...to get away from a man," I replied, smiling and without thinking.

"Where are you from?" he asked.

"Ireland," I replied.

"I know, but what part?"

"Oh, Donegal. Do you know Ireland?"

"Some of it. I have been to Dublin."

As I walked to a seat on the train, I wondered if he would join me. I sat down and he proceeded to sit down in the seat beside me. I was not sure if I should continue to speak to him, as I felt it might make him feel that he had to talk to me instead of reading his paper. It was part of his ritual, to sit down, take off his glasses and put them in his top pocket, and then concentrate on his evening paper, and if he was anything like my husband, the newspaper came first before anything else in the world. To my surprise and delight, he initiated the conversation when we sat down. We talked about the price of houses and flats and the property market in general.

"Do you live in a house or a flat?" I asked him.

"We live in a house," he answered.

I wondered did the 'we' mean, he and his wife, or he and his son, or he and his parents or what. But I did not dare to ask. Probably his wife, I thought. He asked how I liked living in London and how long I had been there. He seemed to have a nice friendly manner and I immediately felt relaxed in his company. I told him that I loved London, especially the restaurants and the theatre, even though I did not get a chance to see any shows. His favourite was *Les Misérables* and he had seen it three times. It was best, he told me, to get the CD of the music, before going to the live performance. Warming to his company, I told him that I liked to play golf and tennis, but had little opportunity to play either since my arrival in London as I was working all the time.

"Oh, you play golf, do you?" he asked.

"Yes, I love it," I replied. "Do you play?"

"Yes, I do, but not very well."

The conversation continued easily until we reached our destination. We talked mainly about sport and health and fitness. It was a lovely journey, and I was sorry when we had to get off the train. Before the train pulled into the station, he said he would look out for some properties in his area and let me know.

"That's very kind of you. Thank you," I replied.

As I walked off to the left and he to the right again, I thought how nice it would be to have a fine man like him to go home to each evening. But, I reckoned, it was probably the last he would think of me. More than likely I would not get the opportunity to speak to him again. I couldn't keep asking him about the train.

During the following week, I was working late and did not get my usual train in the evenings, so I had no opportunity to view the stranger again. That weekend I went to stay with some relatives in the country. While there, I had time to reflect on this man, especially on how nice he seemed. On the whole I was pleased that I had found the courage to talk to a stranger. It proved that I was getting my confidence back at last.

On my return to the office on the following Monday, I felt a mounting excitement when thinking about the train journey home after work. Would he be on the platform again? Would he speak to me? Would I have the courage to speak to him just one more time if he did not initiate the conversation? I couldn't wait for 5 pm.

While in the country, I had taken possession of an old violin, with which I hoped to rekindle my love of playing after a break of several years. When I arrived on the platform I had the violin under my arm. Immediately, I spotted him. I stood in my usual place, and he stood in his. Suddenly, he looked up.

"Hello," he said. "What's that you've got there?"

I explained that I'd been away for the weekend and we began to talk again. As we walked towards the train, the conversation seemed to come naturally. Again he sat down beside me. The conversation somehow turned to life and the stress that it produced. I told him a little of my recent man-related stress.

"Did your white hair come about through similar stress or divorce?" I asked.

"No," he replied. "My wife died of cancer ten years ago." Then he added, "I got married again six months ago."

"Oh, I see," I responded, feeling more than a little disappointed that he was married.

"My hair turned this colour when I had a heart attack two years after she died," he added.

I suddenly felt a great closeness to this man. It seemed that he had been through even more than I had in the past few years. What a pity I had not known him during the time between his wife dying and him meeting his present wife. After a while, I asked if he was going to the gym when he got home. He had mentioned previously that he went every Monday night.

"No, actually I'm going to the driving range tonight. Would you like to come?"

I was slightly taken aback. I presumed he was just being polite.

"Are you going with some friends?" I asked.

"No, just myself. Would you like to join me?"

I didn't know what to say. I had just returned from a hectic weekend. I was hungry, dirty and exhausted. I had planned a hot bath, a quick supper, and then the bliss of bed.

"What time are you going?" I enquired.

"Around 6.30 or 6.45," he replied. "I'll collect you if you like. Where do you live?"

I had to get my wits together and fast. How could I possibly go off somewhere with a total stranger? I knew nothing about him other than the area he lived.

"Okay," I said, "That would be lovely."

My God, what have I done, I thought to myself. I had no idea if I could get a babysitter for my ten-year-old son at such short notice. Of course, I couldn't tell him that, as he had no knowledge of my children. I still don't know why I hadn't mentioned it before. My next thought was where was the location of this driving range? Then I thought what was the use of being so careful all the time. So what if he is an axe murderer, sometimes you have to take the chance, I decided. What had being careful and reserved all my life got me? Nothing. What did I have to lose? I would just have to trust God this time.

As we got off the train, he told me he would see me in half an hour. I had given him directions to my flat, but I wasn't sure if he had fully understood them. Possibly he would not turn up. When I got home, I rang my daughter to see if she could take my son for a couple of hours. The answering machine was on. No one at home. I panicked. What would I do now? I fumbled in the fridge and found some cold pasta which I quickly heated in the microwave. I ran into the bedroom and searched furiously for something appropriate to wear. Nothing was suitable. Eventually, I pulled on my leather trousers and a warm fleece jacket.

Finally, I located my daughter at 6.30 pm.

"Please can you take him for an hour? I'm going for a quick drink with some people from work," I lied.

She would have had a blue fit if she knew what I was up to. Roles had reversed and she was now very protective of me, and worried about me continuously. Next I had to deliver Luke to her house. What would happen if the stranger called in the meantime? He would think I was standing him up. Hurriedly, I scribbled a note which read, *Message for golf person. Back soon. Please wait.* After I had stuck it to the main door, I realised that I did not even know his name, and there I was preparing to drive off into the night with him. I must have been mad.

When I arrived back in the driveway after leaving off my son, I saw a car in the darkness with its parking lights on. Standing by the car was the stranger.

"Sorry to keep you," I said. "Did you get my note?"

"Yes, I did. Thank you. My name is Richard, by the way," he said, extending his hand towards me.

"And I'm Marguerite," I replied. "Yes, I just realised I didn't even know your name when I went to write you the note."

His hand had felt soft and warm, but he had a strong grip. I felt a definite thrill shoot up my arm. I ran upstairs and collected my golf shoes and clubs, more of my treasured possessions taken with me at the time of my flight. On my way through the kitchen, I considered that it might be wise to carry some sharp object in case he attacked me. I looked around and the first thing I saw was a corn-on-the-cob skewer. Well, always be prepared, they say. I put it into my jacket pocket and smiled to myself at the excitement I felt. Out loud I said, "Take a chance, woman."

16

Mercs and Perks, but not for Me

No matter how hard I tried, the memories of my husband's promotion to Cabinet as Minister for Tourism, Sport and Recreation always came rushing back to me. The wonderful happy and proud memories at first, and then the sad ones that followed.

It was Wednesday, 9 July 1997 and we were at Dáil Éireann. All around the house there was a palpable air of tension and expectation. Bertie Ahern was within hours of introducing his new Cabinet to the Dáil. But who were these beings that Bertie was on the verge of elevating to some of the highest offices in the land? No one knew, not even the chosen ones. It was 12.30 pm. All our family were there, crammed into my husband's small office. My daughter and grandson had flown in from London that morning. My three boys were there. My mother-in-law was there, along with my sisters and brothers-in-law. Rumour had abounded that my husband might be in line for one of these fifteen illustrious jobs, so it had seemed only fitting that his family be there to share in his hour of glory, should that honour be bestowed upon him. However, we were all in a cautious if excited frame of mind. Once bitten, twice shy, and all of that.

It was a warm day. James sat behind his desk, trying desperately hard not to eat his hands. The baby slept peacefully on a blanket in the middle of the floor, blissfully unaware of the drama surrounding his grandfather.

Family members sat or stood uneasily, or paced backwards and forwards. Snippets of nervous conversation permeated the tense silence.

"Did you have a good journey up?"

"Big crowd outside."

"Grand day for it."

The thing about situations like this in Leinster House is that no TD trusts his fellow TD. This is the day when it's every man for himself. Watch your backs boys and girls. So it was not a case of one guy picking up his phone and calling a fellow deputy down the hall to say, "Hello, Johnny. Have you heard anything from Bertie yet?"

No, it was a case of each individual sitting tight in his own office waiting for that God-feared phone call from the top. If the phone had rung for any other reason that morning, then we would all most likely have died of fright. Bertie was drawing them out to the last.

Back in 1991, Charlie Haughey had called my husband at 8 pm the previous evening, informing him of his appointment as Minister for Defence, which would be announced officially in the Dáil and to the press the following morning. But in 1997, it was a brand new Dáil which had been elected by the people three weeks earlier, and any number of individuals could have come out winners. Bertie was ensuring that nothing was leaked to the press in advance, so he was playing his cards extremely close to his chest. Not that this did any good to the blood pressure and palpitation of the hopefuls, but certainly it was Bertie's prerogative as incoming Taoiseach.

I looked at my husband and knew instantly that he needed space. He needed peace. I knew that these types of tense situations in his life required him to be on his own. He derived no solace or comfort from those around him. He preferred to wait with just himself for company.

"Why don't we all go over to Buswell's and see if we can get some tea and sandwiches?" I suggested.

"I think James is feeling a bit claustrophobic and maybe needs some time on his own. He can ring us if there's anything to report."

Some were not too sure if he should be left alone, but I knew from the way that he ushered the throng of us out the door that he was relieved.

On such occasions, each TD is allocated two passes to the public gallery overlooking the Dáil chamber. It was unanimously agreed that my mother-in-law and myself would use these two passes. The rest were happy to watch the entertainment on the monitor in my husband's office. Proceedings were due to begin at 3 pm. At 2.30 pm as we waited nervously in Buswell's, I received a call from a FF press officer telling me that Granny and I should make our way to our seats straightaway.

"Why, have you heard something?" I asked nervously.

"I can't say anything, but Jim asked me to give you a call," she replied.

I felt a slight tremor of excitement, but was almost afraid to hope. We took our seats in the gallery and the air there was electric. I had no idea how these events worked until the wife of an ex-minister had spoken to me on the stairs.

"If he doesn't come in and take his seat with the rest of the TDs, then you'll know that he has got something," she said.

It was 2.50 pm and a steady trickle of TDs from all the parties began to filter in and take their seats down below us in the chamber. Granny and I watched with bated breath.

"Please don't come in yet," I prayed silently.

The tension was unbearable. Gradually more and more seats began to fill up. There was no allocated seating that day, so TDs could sit where they chose, within their own party confines, naturally. Fianna Fáilers to the right, Fine Gaelers to the left, and the rest in between. Our eyes scanned the various entrances and the rows of seating. Someone behind me put their hand on my shoulder and said, "It's looking good, he's not in yet."

I began to hope. One thing I knew about my husband was that he was always on time for official occasions. Indeed, he was always early for meetings. I remembered back to when some years earlier as a raw recruit, he was guest speaker at a dinner somewhere in the far reaches of the Kerry countryside one cold winter's evening. *Dinner 8 pm*, the invitation had read.

"Must be on time," he said.

We arrived at the venue at eight on the dot. Not a being in sight.

"Are we in the right place?" he asked me, his driver.

I checked the address on the invitation. Yes, we were in the right place, sure enough. Then out of the darkness a lone figure appeared.

"Oh hello, Dr McDaid. You are very welcome to Kerry."

It was six weeks after 'The McDaid Affair', and he recognised my husband instantly.

"Have we come to the right place for a function this evening?" we asked.

"Ah, yer in the right place all right, but yer a bit early. I would say there won't be anyone here til nearer ten o'clock. I'm just here getting the place ready."

Well, rural Ireland is rural Ireland, and will possibly never change. We went back to our hotel for two hours and almost fell asleep.

But back to Bertie and the Soldiers of Destiny. I knew that if my husband was to sit on the backbenches, then he would be there by now. Then a giant hush descended as Bertie Ahern appeared at the doorway of the chamber. There was a sharp intake of nervous breath. He walked forward, followed by his chosen crew, Brian Cowen, Charlie McCreevy, Michael Woods, Dermot Ahern, and on and on it went. Then, suddenly James appeared. I thought my heart would burst. Granny and I jumped up and hugged each other, she whispering a short prayer, me uttering a few small four-letter words, the way football fans do when Ireland score a goal. The pride and joy we felt for him was unbelievable. Behind us, people were patting us on the back, whispering their congratulations to us. He took his seat on the front bench and I felt I had never loved him more than I did at that moment. I wanted to break the glass, swing over the balcony and jump down and hug him to death.

This was the moment that would make up for all the disappointment he had gone through in 1991. It was the greatest day of his life. I learnt later from my children that their first sign that things were looking good was from the window of my husband's office. A long glass corridor links two of the buildings in Leinster House, and his office window overlooked this corridor. Here they had spotted Bertie walking towards the Dáil chamber with his new Cabinet marching in step behind him. This is when they had spotted Dad in the line-up, but they could not call me on my mobile, as it was switched off in the gallery. So that was how the story unfolded to his nearest and dearest.

Afterwards on the plinth, the photographers were snapping and the microphones were recording. "How do you feel, Minister?" The questions kept coming. But I couldn't get near him. Two hours later in the bar of Buswell's Hotel, I eventually got a chance to congratulate him. I put my arms around him and hugged him and kissed him and told him how proud I was of him. But his body felt like stone, and his eyes just stared coldly and quizzically at me. I put it down to his tiredness and the tension of the past days and weeks. The partying went on well into the night, with the PDs and FF celebrating in unison. Mary Harney was on top of the world, and it was great to see her proud elderly parents arrive to celebrate their daughter's wonderful success.

Fortunately, I had booked rooms for all the family in Buswell's so that we could all enjoy the festivities without having to worry about getting home later. By 2 am, everyone was heading off and I went up to bed, the 'kids' having gone much earlier. My husband said he would be up in a few minutes. He was just saying goodbye to a few people.

At 7 am, the phone by the bed woke me up.

"Good morning Mrs McDaid. This is Highland Radio in Letterkenny. Can we speak to Jim please? We would like to get him on the 8 am news bulletin."

I looked around the room, but there was no one there. My husband had not come to bed. Once again, I got that sinking feeling.

"I'm sorry," I said. "He isn't in this room, I think he might be in one of the boys rooms. I'll find him for you and get him to call you back as soon as possible."

Immediately, I felt that cold hand of fear around my heart again. I knew well he was not in the boy's room, but rang anyway to check, just in case. I was right. They had not seen him. The radio station rang again.

"Oh, I'm sorry. He went out very early, apparently," I lied.

At 10 am we all went down for breakfast.

"Where's Dad?" the 'kids' asked.

"Oh, he had to do an early interview," I lied again. "He'll be back later."

I had been trying my husband's mobile phone since 7 am but there was no reply. By 11 am family and friends had arrived back at Buswell's but there was still no sighting of the new Minister. Even his new Garda driver turned up with the Merc, but with no Minister. And so I lied and fibbed for an hour until eventually he arrived in the foyer.

"Had to go out early to a meeting," he told them.

He said nothing to myself or the kids. They didn't bother to ask. Shortly after his arrival, I spotted him heading for the gents so I followed him.

"Where did you get to last night?" I asked. "Why didn't you stay here?"

He turned on me with a look of pure venom.

"I'm warning you, just don't start making trouble for me," he began. "Where I stay is my business and you better not start interfering. I'm warning you, just don't cause any more trouble."

I went back to the group in the lobby and fought hard to hide my hurt. What had I done? I had only asked a question any wife would ask. Yet still I was the villain. Once again, I decided not to let this incident ruin the day for the kids and for the family, so I swallowed my pride and joined in the jovial mood.

Back in Donegal that night, the bonfires blazed and the car horns hooted. The town band came out and led us up the main street. The crowds gathered in the square and the cheers rang out. On the balcony overlooking the throngs, people nudged me and said, "Smile". But the smile went no further than my face. Inside, I already knew that he had burst my bubble.

The morning after the celebrations, I had a brief chance to speak to him, before the crowds descended on the house again. He was standing in the kitchen making a cup of tea.

"You must be happy now that you've got to the top?" I asked, in a friendly tone. "What do you mean?" he retorted. "This isn't the top. I intend to have Bertie's job. I intend to be Taoiseach."

I groaned inwardly. Would there be no end to it?

17

Days of Wine and Roses

After hitting one hundred balls on the driving range, Richard drove me straight home. Safely. Part of me was a little disappointed that he had not suggested a drink perhaps on the way back. But, after all, he was married. I knew that. Still he was great company and had appeared to enjoy mine in return. As I went to get out of the car, he asked if he might have my telephone number. And, perhaps I would like to join him for a drink some evening after work, while waiting for the train? He suggested the following Thursday. I agreed. I could feel a definite thrill rising up inside me, but had to keep a lid on it.

'He is married. Don't forget that,' a little voice inside me whispered. Yet the prospect of doing something adult, like going for a drink after work, did hold an enormous attraction for me. I was fed up leaving the office every evening, getting on the bus, getting on the Tube, getting on the train and then back to sit in the flat for the rest of the evening. I needed some excitement, even if it was only having a drink. We agreed to meet at 5.30 pm at a wine bar in Victoria and for the rest of that week, I could think of nothing else. Again, I managed to convince my daughter that I was meeting some people from work. Though glad that I was finally socialising again, she was wary.

"Be careful coming home and don't stay out too late," she warned. "Those trains can be dangerous places at that time of night. Make sure you are home by ten at the latest."

God bless her. When had we reversed roles? She was now the mother and I the teenage daughter. We laughed at the craziness of it all.

At 5.30 pm on the dot, I was at the wine bar. No sign of him. I sat for five minutes but it seemed like hours. Again memories of my husband never turning up when he promised began to take over. I feigned deep interest in the newspaper in front of me. The waiter came and asked if I would like a drink, but I indicated that I was waiting for someone. I was actually dying for a drink to settle my nerves but unsure what kind of drinker Richard was. Was he a pint man, a G&T man, a whiskey man, or a coke man? Once again I did not have enough confidence in myself to order what I wanted, just in case he might find me prim and proper with a glass of wine, common with a beer, or stuffy with a sparkling water. What I really needed was a stiff brandy to bolster my courage but if he turned up and found me smelling like a brewery, what might he think? Five more minutes passed and I had nearly given up when I spotted him running. His hair was unmistakable in the crowded thoroughfare.

As he approached the table, I jammed my head back into the *Evening Standard*, trying to look as nonchalant as possible. I looked up just as he approached the table, and nearly fell off my chair when he bent down and kissed my cheek. His apologies were profuse, explaining how his train had been stuck in the tunnel for fifteen minutes. I was just so glad not to have been stood up that I did not care how late he was.

"What would you like to drink?" he asked.

"I don't know really, what are you having?" I said.

"How about a nice bottle of white wine?" he suggested.

You could have knocked me over with a feather, as they say. A man to share a bottle of wine with at 5.30 pm on a Thursday evening at a wine bar in London. My God, I had really died and gone to heaven. And on top of all that, he was gorgeous. Two hours later we were still deep in conversation, and the wine bottle was empty. I expected him to say okay we best go and catch our train. After all, he had a wife at home. To my surprise and delight, he suggested we have something to eat. I did not object. He called for some menus and asked me if I would like some more wine. Does a cat like milk? So he ordered another bottle. Later that evening the taxi pulled up outside my flat and he offered me his hand to climb out. He asked if perhaps we could do it again another time. Then he kissed me on the cheek and bade me goodnight.

I sailed up those three flights of stairs as if on a cushion of air. We had gelled from the moment he had sat down. He was interested in me as a person. He was interested in everything I said. He was even interested in my opinions. And, the feeling was mutual. For the first time in years, I began to feel like a real person.

But underlying all of this was a deep mistrust. From somewhere in the back of my mind came a fixation that he had somehow been planted in my path for some political reason. To catch me out in some way. It took weeks and months for me to believe what he was telling me. When he told me where he lived, I said that for all I knew he might not live there at all, but in a hut in the back garden. The whole thing in my head was so bizarre. I was obsessed with the idea that my husband was somehow involved in our meeting. Maybe this was why I unfortunately succeeded in pushing to the back of my mind the fact that he was married. Maybe I believed that nothing would come of it, so I had nothing to worry about. We would go our separate ways eventually. So what was wrong with enjoying meals in nice restaurants in the West End? Or bottles of wine in beautiful wine bars? No one had ever treated me this well before, so I might as well make the most of it. We were simply enjoying each other's company. And it certainly beat trudging home to a dull flat every night of the week. My daughter was delighted that I was getting out a bit from work, and looked after Luke without any problem. I dared not tell her the truth, even though she was keen for me to meet a nice man at some stage in the future. Not a married one, however.

Gradually, over the following weeks, I noticed a change in myself. A strange softening in my head perhaps. Could it be that I was starting to heal? Could it be that this wonderful kind and caring man was gently applying a type of soothing, healing balm to my severely lacerated brain? Were the scars beginning to fall off, leaving some healthy tissue underneath? Was I at last beginning to contemplate that there possibly could be a future for me on this earth. Maybe, just maybe, there could be some happiness out there for me.

Eventually Richard told me the story of how his wife had died, leaving him to bring up his two children, then aged fourteen and eleven. His life had been tough. Having been forced to sell his engineering business, he took a job with a company that offered more regular hours but less hassle and stress so he could spend time with his children. He was a committed father and his children were his priority. Eight years later, with his children able to cope for themselves, he felt lonely. Various friends had tried to match him up, but he had never met anyone suitable. Then one day he saw an advertisement for an introduction agency and decided to take the plunge. The first three were totally unsuitable, ranging from a vegetable farmer – who lived at home with her ageing father – to an artist, who turned up for their date, covered in paint.

By the time he got to number four, he decided that he better try and make a go of it with her. At the time she seemed amiable, and they began to go out on dates. Then she suggested they sell both their houses and buy one between them. He agreed, but wasn't too bothered. Then she suggested they get married. In his own words, he figured this was his lot, and he didn't want to grow old all alone. Well, none of us do. He reckoned that his chances of meeting someone he loved second time around were well over, so against his better judgement, he agreed to get married. That was just six short months before we met at Victoria. Before the ink was dry on the wedding certificate, she had started to take less pride in her appearance, much to his dismay. She refused to allow him display any photographs or mementoes of his late wife in their house. Everything had to be packed away in the attic or gotten rid of altogether. She did allow him to keep some of his exquisite furniture, however. But she fell out with his son and had a strained relationship with his beloved daughter. He was absolutely miserable and unhappy. He knew that he had made a terrible mistake, but was stuck. What could he do? He did not love her. He doubted if she loved him either. She bossed him about and never let him out of her sight. The marriage was truly a disaster.

Every day, I told myself to finish the relationship. The last thing I needed was to get involved with a married man. But how could I bring myself to cut myself off from my supply of energy and love? It would be like cutting off my oxygen supply. I needed this man. I needed to be cared for. No one had ever cared for me since I had left my parents house twenty-nine years earlier. Certainly not my husband. He had never asked me how I was feeling. He had never asked me what kind of day I had. Now here was someone who pampered me, called me at work to see how I was, bought me flowers, perfume, chocolates. He opened doors for me, walked on the outside of the footpath, came shopping with me, and genuinely looked happy every time we met. How could I tell him to go away? I couldn't. I was weak. Richard showed me respect, understanding, compassion and all of those other things which made me feel so strongly towards him. He would have cut off his right hand rather than hurt me. But, unfortunately, he was not on the transfer list. And would never be.

18

On the Move Again

All good things must come to an end. Just as we were getting on our feet, the owner of our flat returned from abroad and wanted her property back. It was now almost one year since we had left Ireland and gradually I was learning to take some risks.

My daughter and her husband were bringing their little boy to Disneyland in Florida that spring and suggested we come with them. She offered to lend me some of the money, and I took the big step of borrowing the remainder from a lending agency. It had been a long hard year, and I felt that a break would do us the world of good. Since he was a toddler my son had always asked if Daddy and I would take him to Disney some day and I had always reassured him that we would try. Down through the years when my older children had asked, I had fobbed them off with a promise of 'we'll take you when you are older'. Now they were all grown up and gone, and we had never had that magical opportunity. I was determined not to leave it until too late with Luke.

On the day I moved out of the flat, the owner treated me with utter disdain. I still do not understand her reasoning, as I had neither spoken nor contacted her since the day I had moved in. I had made no complaints or asked for anything for the flat. I had, in fact, been the ideal tenant. We were due to depart for Florida that morning and the taxi was waiting at my daughter's house to take us to the airport. Again I had to endure the famous inventory, while she counted the egg cups, plates and so on. While she inspected every inch of the place, I had to hang around waiting for the return of my deposit. Finally, she turned to me.

"I am withholding £90 of your deposit because the kitchen floor has not been washed properly," she informed me. "Your contract states that you must leave my flat in the condition you found it. I will need to hire a cleaner to come in and clean it after you."

I was aghast. I looked at the grubby lino on the floor, which was twenty-years-old at least, and had never in all the time I was there managed to look clean. It had certainly not been clean on the day I moved in. However, I refused to let her get the better of me. Livid with anger, I marched into the kitchen. I grabbed a bucket and cloth and got down on my knees and scrubbed the floor, while she sat there watching me. No way was she getting my hard-earned ninety pounds.

When I had finished I was dripping in sweat and my lovely new holiday clothes ruined, but I did get my full deposit back. I felt totally and utterly humiliated. Certainly, I was halfway over the Atlantic Ocean before the rage began to wear off and I could begin to enjoy my holiday. My daughter had been on the verge of going back to hit the old crow, but I convinced her it was not worth it. She was angry because she had spent the previous two days cleaning my flat, just in case the owner had any complaints. And having lived in flatland since her college days, she was used to these sharks.

Before leaving our first flat, I had begun the long and arduous process of finding us another new home. Each day at work, I would ring the different letting agencies to see what was on offer. At least this time when they asked if I was employed, I could confidently answer, "Yes." This time they even had to have confirmation of my exact annual income. After work I would view what was on offer. Rental accommodation was in high demand, so I was left with very little choice. Of course, there were dozens of beautiful flats on offer in salubrious surroundings, but my meagre budget didn't stretch that far. I saw flats with balconies, with working lifts, with gardens, with managers to oversee the property, and even one with an en suite bathroom. But they were for people who had money, and I was not one of those lucky punters. Once again like in the early days, I could feel the desperation and panic setting in. I could not possibly impose on my daughter and son-in-law once again. The other terrifying prospect was that I might have to return to Ireland.

Eventually, I found something that I thought would do us. It was within ten minutes walk of the railway station, which was always a bonus when commuting to London. It was described as a 'conversion' on the third floor of an old Georgian house. A conversion, I learned, was a large house which had been turned into three or four individual properties, all using a common entrance and staircase. I met the letting agent outside the property at 7 pm that evening. My first instinct was to run as far away as possible. If time could go back one hundred years, it would have been paradise. A beautiful tree-lined avenue with tall elegant palatial private residences. Castellated roofs, giant bay windows, vast colonnaded entrance porches. However, this was 1999 and just a century too late. By now the lawn to the front had been replaced with concrete. It was cracked and sunken, with weeds growing knee-high from the crevices. This was now the car park. 'Off-street parking', i.e. in the front garden, is regarded of course as another major bonus in London. When the letting agent had boasted about off-street parking, I had naively imagined something totally different.

The grand front door had long lost its lustre and was now in some danger of coming off its hinges. Its once stained-glass portals were now replaced with plywood panels. Inside the long broad hallway, three bicycles were chained to a radiator. Even inside this haven of safety, one bicycle had been deprived of its wheels. The stairs leading to the flat for rent was covered in threadbare carpet, with gaping holes in the risers. It was reminiscent of houses many years ago, when the steps of the stair carpet became worn, the entire carpet was raised a few inches, so that the unworn part from the previous riser became the base for the following step above it. I expected to see giant mice and rats peeping out at me from the holes. In the ensuing months, I never walked those stairs but ran for my life each time. Looking on the bright side, I became very fit.

In the year since I had arrived in London, the price of rental property had skyrocketed. Unfortunately, my salary had not escalated at an equal rate. I seemed to be continuously stressed about money. I was like Scrooge doling it out, and having endless arguments with my son every time he needed money for school trips or new football boots or any of the other million things that young boys need. It was unfair on him. The best way I could think of cutting down on our monthly outgoings was to rent a one-bedroom flat, instead of the two bedrooms we had up to then. I was totally aware that this would not be an ideal situation for either of us, and that any privacy I now had would be gone. He and I were also aware that this would cut out any chance he had of having his friends sleep over at weekends. However, as usual he did not complain, and actually looked forward to having nice long chats each night before going to sleep.

The flat itself didn't actually look too bad. It was spacious, bright and airy, the living room having a giant bay window looking out over the treetops. It was decorated in bright modern colours with splashes of oranges and yellows and lilacs. On that bright April evening, it seems just what we were looking for, to cheer us up.

And of course the *pièce de résistance,* a huge big waterbed. I knew immediately that this would swing it with Luke. If I had shown him the place from the outside, without the carrot of the waterbed, I knew he would be somewhat put off, to say the least. Such excitement when I went home and told him. He couldn't wait to move in.

Unfortunately, the flat would not be available until May, thus leaving us with a two-week gap between the end of the lease on my first abode and the commencement of the second. I could only take possession on return from our holiday, so there was nothing for it but to pack everything we owned into my car once again, only this time the bulk of our belongings had expanded threefold. And so the car was parked in the street for two weeks, with everything we possessed, packed roof high inside the car, driver's seat included. It was miraculous that the car was not stolen during those two weeks, but then again, who would bother? Would anyone really want to go to the trouble of pulling all that junk out of there just for a joyride? Probably not, I hoped, as I lay on the beach in Florida, trying desperately to relax. After a wonderful two weeks in America, it was back to London and back to reality. Arriving at Gatwick Airport in the early morning, exhausted with jet lag, I dreaded the thought of what lay ahead that day.

Fortunately, no one had stolen my car, so after clearing a space on the driver's seat, I set off for the letting agency to collect the keys of my new home. Before I left for Florida, I had arranged for the telephone at the new place to be connected in my name. By some miracle and feat of strength, I managed to haul the entire contents of my life up three flights of stairs and into my flat. With my fiftieth birthday approaching the following week and my jet lag overtaking me, I'm not quite sure how I managed it. The rest of the family had gone home to bed, and pleaded with me to leave the moving until the following day, but I just wanted to get it over with. I needed a base as soon as possible. Anyway, I thought, once I get everything cleared from the car, I can climb onto the waterbed and go to sleep. Task completed, I then proceeded to lock my front door. Big problem. The key would not turn in the lock. It seemed like a new set that had been cut, and obviously had some minor imperfection. As luck would have it, this was the only means of even keeping the door closed, let alone locked. I reached for the phone to ring the letting agent. Dead telephone. It had not been connected. I reached for my mobile. It had been in the car for two weeks, and the battery was dead.

I was stuck. It was midday. The sun was splitting the stones outside and inside the temperature was rising. I desperately wanted to go to bed and sleep, but could not with the door lying wide open. That action in such a location would be foolhardy. I could be murdered in my waterbed by an intruder, as I slept. If I went out to search for a public phone, my flat could be robbed. Then, totally by accident, I discovered that the key did work from the outside. Eventually, my only option was to drive to the letting agency and enlist their help. What a mistaken belief that turned out to be. I drove there like a woman possessed, and explained my plight. It was now 2 pm and sleep depravation was beginning to take a firm hold of my brain. Were they interested in my story? Not a bit of it. As far as they were concerned, they had kept their part of the deal and supplied me with the keys to gain entry to the flat. We had signed the agreement and I had handed over my £100 agent's fee. They also had one month's rent in advance, plus my deposit of the equivalent of one month's rent to cover damages. A total of £1,300.

It was now between myself and the owner of the property, they said. Now where I wonder, had that sweet smiling gentlemanly letting agent gone? The same man who only three short weeks before had promised me the earth, moon and stars. Any problems, he had said, 'you come straight to me.' Except the 'me' now referred to an unsympathetic, uncaring slimeball who was only interested in his next unsuspecting customer. They did, however, offer an extremely helpful suggestion.

"Perhaps you should drive up to North London where the property owner lives, and see if he has a spare set of keys."

How amusing. North London was a four-hour drive away, and I hadn't a clue how to get there.

Despite thirty minutes of protestations on my part, they shrugged off all responsibility. I sat in my car on the street and once again, cried. I cried tears of exhaustion, frustration, injustice and hopelessness. Where was I going to spend the night? My daughter's house was full with sleeping relations. I found a public phone and rang the owner.

"Sorry. Nothing I can do," he said.

He was busy at work and asked was I sure that I had put the key properly in the lock? Had I tried pushing the door as I turned the key? I could just hear his mind going, 'Stupid cow. Can't even turn a key in a lock. Women!' It would be Sunday before he could possibly get down with a replacement set of keys. It was now Wednesday. What was I going to do in the meantime.

I had to get some sleep. I just had to close my eyes. As it stood then, I could barely see the road ahead. I was a driving hazard. But I succeeded in navigating my way back to the flat, getting lost several times en route. Finally, I pulled a heavy box over behind the front door, and climbed into bed. I did not really care at that stage if someone did come in and murdered me. In fact, I would have considered it a relief. It would save me having to do it myself. And at least then, no one could put the blame on me. Could I sleep? Not a chance. My mind was doing a combination of the Grand National, the Grand Prix at Silverstone, and the London Marathon all at the same time. And after a two-hour struggle, I gave up.

I was standing in the living room waiting for the kettle to boil when a knock came to my door. I froze in terror. In the year I had spent in London, we had one cardinal rule. *Never, ever open the front door unless expecting someone.* I knew if it were one of the family, they would have called out my name. Now here I was defenceless, without even a locked door between myself and some total stranger, who could be a madman. I forced myself not to move a muscle. I knew the living room had some creaky floorboards and if I stood on one, I was a gonner. Then I listened in disbelief as I heard a key being inserted into the lock. My knees were weak and I hoped that I had actually fallen asleep after all and it was some horrible nightmare. The sweat poured from my body. I could hear the intruder trying to turn the key, then discovering it was unlocked. I saw the shadow of the door being pushed slowly open. This is it. This is definitely it. Please God, please make it quick and painless. Please don't let him rape me. I closed my eyes and waited.

"Oh, Mrs McDaid, you are here. Remember me. I'm sorry to disturb you."

My eyes flashed open. It was the young man who had rented the flat before me. I had met him and his partner the evening I came to view the flat, and they had seemed a very pleasant young couple.

"We had some spare sets of keys that I thought you might need, so I was passing and thought I better drop them in to you."

I could hardly believe what I was hearing. Not only had I not been murdered in cold blood, but also this angel from heaven had even a set of keys that worked, I hoped. I recounted my tale of the past couple of hours to him.

"Oh yes," he replied. "We had trouble with that set of keys months ago and gave them back to the estate agent. They never worked."

I felt a mounting fury overcome me. Those inhumane sharks in the letting agency had been aware that the key was faulty in the first place. But once I had signed the form to say I had received the keys, that was them out of the equation. I decided there and then that they hadn't heard the last of me. Definitely not. Of course, the fact that very few things in the flat actually worked did not help matters either. The intercom on the hall door downstairs did not work, so I had no way of knowing who was ringing the doorbell, when the bell was working, that is.

"Don't worry, you are perfectly safe here," was the consolation I got from the owner. "No one here has ever been broken into yet."

I was not interested in becoming a statistic. *Woman and child murdered in first ever break-in at Sydenham Road*, the headlines would scream. But, the landlord did not want to know. Why had I not checked all these things before I agreed to take the flat? For the simple fact that working full time and flat hunting do not go hand in hand, I told myself. I was desperate to put a roof over our heads and had no time to look any further. Naively, I had believed the nice man at the letting agency. Next time, however, if I survived till next time, I would be a lot more careful.

After the young man left, I managed to lie down and close my eyes for an hour. It was at this stage that I was able to relax a little and contemplate my new waterbed. One of the downsides about my trip to America was that it had meant an enforced absence from Richard, and there was plenty of truth in the saying that absence makes the heart grow fonder and all of that. We were both eagerly awaiting a wonderful reunion due at 6 pm that evening. Well, at least now I had the keys and felt safe enough to have a shower, wash my hair and try to wake myself up and look radiant. Thankfully, I had a wonderful golden Florida tan to hide the pallor of my debilitating jet lag.

At six on the dot, I heard him call up from the street through my open window. My Prince Charming serenading me on the balcony of my castle. Well, not quite. The doorbell didn't work, he informed me. What a surprise! But there he was, his arms filled with wine, flowers and *The Telegraph*. He always brought me his copy to read. It was like a scene from *Romeo and Juliet* as I rushed downstairs and into his waiting arms, or something like that. I was never so happy to see anyone in my life. He was my rock. He would sooth the stress of the last eight hours. But he had never seen the flat before and I was terrified that he would think that I was a complete nutter for having chosen such a kip. I kept his attention diverted from the chained up bicycles and the mice peeping out from the staircase, and led him up to my humble dwelling. He was pleasantly surprised, and I was delighted at his reaction.

"Yes, it could be very nice," he said.

Once he noticed my face darken at his first comment, he added, "I'm sure it will be just lovely once you put your own expert touches to it."

Anyway, nothing mattered other than the fact that we were together again. As I had not much success in sleeping on the waterbed earlier in the day, it seemed only prudent that one should make another attempt at this Everest, and this time with some help. Well, after all, someone had to give it its driving test, and the sooner the better.

While in America, I had come across some beautiful satin bed linen in Macy's. I just couldn't resist them. Pink satin sheets, just like Marilyn Monroe had. It was something I had hankered after for years, as my mother, who had lived in the US for many years, had told me about the joy of slipping in between soft silky slippery satin sheets and feeling like a princess or a movie star. All the way back on the plane the previous night, I had dreamed about the combination of satin sheets and waterbed. I had never actually slept on a waterbed before, but I was reliably informed that it would be sheer heaven. So how could things be any more perfect? Satin, water and the man of my dreams. Perfection, in other words. Three hours later, our bodies ached from laughter. It was soon discovered that the combination of satin and water, washed down by a few glasses of Chianti, culminated in something equivalent to being in a small inflatable dinghy in fifty-foot waves, somewhere twenty miles north of the coast of Donegal in the wild Atlantic Ocean. Suffice it to say that docking procedures were severely hampered by the continuous undulating movement of the waters in the vicinity. This combined with the extremely slippery satin surface underfoot, resulted in one hanging on for dear life to anything within grasping range, the greatest danger coming from the threat of sliding overboard onto the hard and unyielding wooden floor below. Eventually, an exhausted defeat was declared on all sides, and there was nothing for it but to finish the remains of the wine and read *The Telegraph!*

After a few weeks in the flat, my son and I began to settle in again, and he gained many hours of innocent enjoyment messing about on the waterbed. He loved it. I, however, got up every morning feeling slightly seasick. One weekend I invested in a few DIY tools and managed to fix most of the non-working items myself. Like the toilet that would not flush, for instance. I even managed to fit a new ball cock, which was something I had not done in my previous life. Another thing I managed to secure was the piece of kitchen cupboard that fell down on my head each time I attempted to open the oven door. I also fixed the leaky tap in the kitchen, which had been letting all my expensive hot water run down the drain. And I even fixed the wardrobe door, which had come off in my hand on the first occasion I opened it. Meanwhile I was working full-time, trying to be a good mother, trying to make ends meet financially, and dragging my jaded body up and down three flights of dingy stairs.

Fortunately, outside the sun was shining and the climate warm and dry. Again that summer, I longed for my lovely home in Donegal and my garden, but I had to force all such thoughts out of my mind. The flat had been advertised as having a communal back garden, but I soon discovered that I had to escape through a heavily bolted door, climb over six overflowing garbage cans, duck under barbed wire and then

Above: Family holiday in Salthill, 1953.

Below: Proud parents, Paddy and Helen, on Marguerite's First Communion Day, 1956.

Left: Marguerite behind the bar at The Hoop, London, 1968.

Middle: Teen spirit – sisters Nuala, Marguerite and Terri with mother Helen (centre left).

Bottom Left: A 'ciggie' break at The Hoop, 1968.

Bottom Right: London fashion hits Galway, 1968.

Above: College sweethearts – Marguerite and James in 1970.

Below: Wedding Day, 1970.

Below: Awaiting the arrival of his first grandchild, Marguerite's father Paddy with Marguerite and James.

Above: Mother and Child, 1970.

Above: Marguerite and James at the UCG Medical Ball in 1972.

Above: Fully-fledged doctor – James with Marguerite and mother-in-law, Helen, following his medical conferring at UCG in 1974.

*Above: Christmas celebrations –
Marguerite and James, 1982.*

*Above: First Communion Day 1979 for
Garret McDaid.*

Above: Meeting the Boss – James and Charles J. Haughey in 1992.

Above: Marguerite and James with Mary O'Rourke in 1993.

Below: On the campaign trail in Donegal – Marguerite and James with Taoiseach, Mr Bertie Ahern, in 1993.

Above: Kitchen Cabinet – Bertie Ahern in talks with Luke McDaid in 1993.

Below: First-time grandmother – Marguerite with Cameron in 1997.

Above: Luke and Marguerite at Wimbledon in 1995.

Below: Proud grandmother – Marguerite with Jack, Dominic and Cameron in 2002.

sunbathe in six feet of weeds and wild grass. Hardly worth the effort you might say.

Eventually, as I had feared, the waterbed burst. No, I did not attack it with a sharp object. My son actually loved it, even though I did not appreciate the fact that each morning he had somehow managed to slide underneath my body. A truly amazing feat of genius. Mercifully, the 1,200 gallons of water did not flow in torrents onto the floor immediately, engulfing the unsuspecting tenants in the flat below. No, it was more akin to a continuous steady leak really. It manifested itself in the following fashion. Each night I had noticed that my feet became very cold at approximately 4 am. I would then curl them up under me and remain in that position until it was time to get up. On making the bed, I would notice that the section of the sheet at the foot of the bed was slightly damp. I put it down to condensation perhaps. However, it soon became evident that a puddle was forming on the wooden base under the water-filled mattress, and this was seeping up through the sheet as I slept.

It is extremely scientific how a waterbed works. The large volume of liquid had to be heated before you could climb in and go to sleep. So there was an electrically controlled heating system, with a thermostat that maintained the water at a constant comfortable temperature throughout the night.

Unfortunately, because of the leak, and the risk of being electrocuted in our sleep, I had to unplug the thermostat. Water and electricity do not make good bedfellows. This naturally meant that the temperature of the water was out of control, and consequently dropped to zero, or below, depending on the weather. I do not need to describe the feeling of spending the night lying awake on a very big bag of very very cold water. Naturally, I contacted the owner once again.

"Can't you empty it, and get an ordinary spring mattress?" he queried.

My God. Would this man not take any responsibility for his premises? I laughingly pictured myself taking two weeks off work and standing there twenty-four hours a day with a bucket, walking back and forth to the window as I emptied my pail onto unsuspecting pedestrians below.

The following day at work was spent phoning waterbed companies and finding out how to empty leaking products. Naturally they were very interested in filling new ones, but less than enthusiastic about emptying old ones. Well, there is very little profit in used water these days. Eventually, I found a willing volunteer and passed on the good news to the owner of the flat.

"Someone will have to be here between 9 am and 6 pm on Friday to let him in," I informed the unhappy soul.

"Okay, that's fine. Go ahead and have it emptied," he replied.

"I'm sorry, but there's no way I can afford to give up a day's pay to sit here and wait for a tradesman," I told him. "You'll have to arrange that yourself."

By that stage, I was at the end of my rope. I had endured his indifference for two months and now I had enough. Eventually, he was left with no option but to make himself available, but this was only after I had threatened him with a letter from my solicitor. I returned from work on the evening of Operation Water to find the wave machine departed and in its place a conventional mattress, with all the signs of having fallen off the back of a lorry in North London. The original waterbed had been of the five-foot variety, and now in its place was a three-foot, six-inch mattress sitting in a five-foot wooden base. This meant that there was a nine-inch gap on all sides, which in turn meant that I could not sit on the side of the bed to get in, but first of all had to climb into the 'coffin' and then lever myself onto the mattress in the centre.

"Why is God doing this to me?" I asked night after night, as I whacked my shins off the edges of the box in my exhausted state. "Why can't he just give me a break?"

I was getting more and more stressed as the weeks progressed and one problem after another presented itself. For a start there was the noise factor. On the floor above, they liked bongo music. Each evening at 9 pm, it would start. One could not hear the tune, but one could not escape the beat. It pounded into my head at intervals, resembling Chinese water torture. By then, I had lost the will to complain. I knew by the look and the strut of the tenants that my pleas for peace and quiet at night would fall on deaf ears. Should I contact the owner? Why waste the price of a phone call? I had taken a six-month tenancy and would lose my deposit if I pulled out before the end of that term. For sure, a £600 deposit was a lot more than I could afford to lose. And I was still only three months into the lease.

It was now August and I was stuck there until November. At least in the bright summer evenings with the sun shining through the front window, one could feel slightly upbeat. But what would it be like on a cold wintry evening? I had not even bothered to test the heating system, but if the rest of the shambles was any indication for me, then most likely it would not be working. I just had to get out of there. On top of all that, it was totally unsuitable for my son and I to be sharing a bed at this stage of his life, let alone sharing a bedroom. So I devised a plan of annoying the landlord to such an extent that he would be relieved to get rid of me as his tenant. This way, hopefully I would not lose my deposit. My plan worked and within three weeks he was so tired of my phone calls and letters that he gave me my notice. I was delighted. Free from that vermin hellhole.

Of course, this meant I was off on the hunt once again. This time, I decided that living in a one-bedroom flat was just not on anymore. I was going to have to find someplace where we could each have some privacy. My son just loved having his friends around to sleep over at weekends, but that was impossible in our present situation. In fact it was impossible for him even to have them over during the day, as he was desperately embarrassed about sharing a bed with his mother. How would he explain when they asked to see his computer or his Playstation in the bedroom? And still he never complained. Sometimes he would say to me, "Mum, sometime when we get enough money to buy a house, can I have a room of my own?" I assured him that the day would come pretty soon, even though I knew in my heart of hearts that I was a million miles from being able to afford anything even close to the house we had been forced to abandon in Donegal.

So I started my search for rented accommodation with as much enthusiasm as going to the gallows. Would the day ever come I wondered, when I could at last unpack my bags permanently. The local paper in areas such as ours contains pages and pages of accommodation for rent. *Two bedroom flat. All mod cons. GFCH. DG. 1st Floor. Garage. Rent £1,000 PCM.* Perfect, but where was I going to get that kind of money? Everything habitable with two bedrooms was out of my league. For £700 I could get a half-decent one bedroom flat in a half-decent location. So what to do? Could my son and I continue to share a bed for the next six months? For the next year? Until he left home? He was now a well-developed eleven-year-old, whose conversations with his friends appeared to centre mainly on the pubescent girls in the adjoining school. None of this was fair on him. But I had no money and therefore no choice.

So once again, I packed the boot of my trusty old Mazda with its steadily expanding precious cargo. I was now getting very tired of packing and unpacking and trying to get used to sleeping in strange beds. I thought of my lovely house at home in Donegal and wished I could just move it over to London. Also, the temptation to give up and return to it was extremely appealing. But my head and my heart were nowhere ready for that. Would they ever be, I wondered?

19

Sound of Silence

*S*o once again, we were back camping out at my daughter's house until we found a new flat. While staying there, I was delighted to be able to spend more time with my adorable little grandson, Cameron. He was now almost two-years-old and loved the Teletubbies. He was sitting on my knee and I was pointing to the various characters in the book, where his favourite Teletubby was La La.

"Look at La La," I repeated over and over again.

Up to this point, Cameron had not much to say for himself. He could, however, manage to get our attention by making a series of sounds. I also repeated a lot of 'Baba', 'Mama' and 'Dada' when I was around him. He did not look at me when I was speaking, and I suspected that his attention span wasn't very long.

After several hearing tests were conducted, we were to learn that he had no hearing at all in his right ear, and just a minimal amount in the left ear. He was profoundly deaf.

My own response to the diagnosis, after the tears, was action. I immediately set about getting my hands on any reading material I could in order to find out more. By sheer chance, I noticed the address and phone number of the National Deaf Children Society (NDCS) in London, and I rang them. I came off the phone from their helpline two hours later, feeling like a weight had been lifted and I was rearing to go. The lady I had spoken to had been so kind and understanding and had listened to all my fears and answered my questions. Armed with a list of addresses and phone numbers, I set to work finding out as much as

I could about deafness and the problems it presented. Some weeks later, I visited their office in London, where I spent many hours being shown around their demonstration area which had all the aids one can imagine, like flashing doorbells, flashing telephones and loop systems to enable the child to listen to the radio and watch TV with the rest of the family.

We came to realise that deafness is more than just not being able to hear. It is far more complex. How do we explain to Cameron, for instance, that the aeroplane that took him to Disneyworld last April was the same thing that he waved at from the garden every day, as the planes flew in and out of nearby Gatwick Airport?

I began to think back to a journey made to Donegal when he was a baby. Around the time Cameron was ten-months-old, his parents experienced great difficulties in getting him a reliable childminder. They rang me two weeks before Christmas saying that the lady who was minding him had been in bad health and was no longer able to care for him. They were desperate and did not know what to do. I suggested that they send Cameron to me in Donegal for the two weeks, as they all planned to come home for Christmas anyway. My husband was due to attend a dinner in London and was flying home to Ireland the following Sunday evening. I suggested that they ask him to take Cameron with him. They agreed.

At 10 pm that Sunday night, grandfather and baby arrived in Donegal, in the company of the ministerial Garda driver. The baby was fine but both men were rather exhausted. Two bags and one buggy were deposited in the hallway. I looked through the bags for Cameron's clothes to get him ready for bed. I found one bag with toys, and the other with food and nappies.

"Where are his clothes?" I asked my husband.

"She said they're in the green case," he replied.

"What green case?" I asked.

There was no green case. The driver and himself dashed forwards and backwards between the house and the boot of the car. No green case could be found. The Minister blamed the driver and I am sure the driver felt like blaming the Minister!

Apparently, baby's mother had warned grandfather at Heathrow, not to give baby his bottle until the plane was about to take off. The sucking sensation would help his ears. Minister was not paying attention to his daughter, naturally enough, and gave bottles to baby once they sat down on the plane. By take-off, all three bottles had been consumed and baby's ears were ringing. Baby never stopped crying. As plane came in to land, baby deposited his three-bottle load all over Minister's bespoke three-piece suit as he sat unsuspecting in the front row of the aircraft's business class. Eventually, a dishevelled Minister and baby made it through customs at Belfast Airport, dragging one buggy and three bags. Immediately, frustrated Minister handed crying baby to terrified driver (i.e. inexperienced childminder), who then placed baby on the floor. Baby immediately attempted to make his escape on all fours, and refused to stay put while driver picked up bags. Minister was by then deep in conversation on his mobile phone, oblivious to driver's difficulty. Confusion reigned supreme. A hasty retreat ensued to the car.

Four hours later, following frantic phone calls to Belfast Airport, we discovered that an unidentified green case had been found sitting on the floor of the arrivals area. By some miracle, the entire contents of Cameron's wardrobe did not end up in a controlled explosion at Belfast International.

Next morning, St Bernard came to the rescue. I popped down to my local for a three-pack of babygros and vests. I did not tell the baby's mother or father that their darling baby boy had gone to bed dressed in a beautiful bright pink outfit, which was a present for a neighbour's baby girl. The following day, the case arrived safely in Donegal.

However, on a more serious note, two days after he arrived, Cameron became unwell. He became very drowsy and continuously fell asleep on my knee, even after he had just woken up. Over those two days he developed a very high temperature. I rang his grandfather, our resident GP, in Dublin and asked for advice.

"He'll be fine," came the reply.

I did not tell his parents in London, as there was no point in worrying them. Cameron had no rash during that time, but later in the week – the day his parents arrived for Christmas – he developed one on his body and his form began to improve. We joked that he had gone through the worst part of the chickenpox while they were in London, and now that they had arrived, he just had the rash for evidence. I had experienced the hardest part with him, I joked. He recovered and was back in form within hours.

In subsequent years, Cameron has gone from strength to strength, enjoying life as all children do and clearly not set back by his hearing difficulties.

20

Third Time Unlucky

While staying at my daughter's house, it was time to go flat hunting once more. Flat No. 3 was, I thought, perfect, even if it had only one bedroom. This time we had a maisonette, a fancy term for a flat with its own front door. What a luxury. No more struggling up three flights of stairs with shopping, heavy school bags and laundry. The fact that it was no bigger than a shoebox and that cat swinging was inadvisable was not important. It was clean and modern and we could park outside our own front door instead of fifty yards down the street. It even had a burglar alarm. And it had its very own back garden. The next summer we would be able to sit out and have barbecues. Perhaps I might even invest in some flower pots and grow some shrubs. More luxury.

But how wrong could I be? Three weeks later as winter set in early and we tried the heating system, we were in for a shock. It didn't work. On the bright September day that we moved in, heating was not an immediate priority. The heaters were in good working order, I was told. Storage heaters in the living room and bedroom, with electric wall heaters in the tiny kitchen and bathroom.

"Storage heating is much cheaper to run than gas heating," the agent assured me.

"Stores the heat at low rates and lets it out when you want it," he raved. "Place lovely and warm when you come in from work in the evening."

Satisfaction guaranteed. Lovely man. Lovely wife. Offered me a coffee while I sat in their letting office discussing the terms of the lease.

"Any problems, you just pick up the phone," he suggested, "and either my wife or myself will be ready to sort them out or any queries you might have."

He was Greek. He looked a bit like Omar Sharif. She resembled Nana Mouskouri. What lovely helpful people. I trusted them implicitly. Well, I had to trust someone.

The owner of the property was a mature lady who had retired to the coast with her husband, and would be in the vicinity on a regular basis. So should any problems arise, she was readily available. Well, she wasn't the actual owner, but managed the property for her son who was abroad. And she sounded extremely pleasant when *she* interviewed *me* over the phone the previous week. She had to 'vet' me to ensure that I was a suitable tenant. Well, landlords have to be careful after all. They don't want to let any old scum into their property. However, once I had signed on the dotted line, paid my £700 deposit, £700 rent in advance for one month and £100 agent's fee, taken the key and walked out of the office, Zorba the Greek and his missus turned into Attila the Hun and whatever crony he hung around with. Thus began one of the worst nightmares and one of the most frightening episodes I was to encounter in all my time in Britain.

To begin with, the door on the freezer compartment of the fridge came off in my hand. The TV aerial only picked up three channels. I would need a special aerial on the roof if I required anything further. At my expense, of course. The actual kitchen itself, I discovered on closer inspection and too late, was covered in a deep layer of transparent grime. The oven was filthy, encrusted with the charred remains of the previous occupant perhaps. The burglar alarm was dysfunctional and no one could locate the key or the code for it. And surprise, surprise, come winter, as I said, the heating did not work. No, I tell a lie. The storage heater in the bedroom did give out some warmth – equivalent to one large candle! And these were just the small things.

For two freezing months, I haggled with the estate agents and the owners, who made some feeble attempts to send a totally useless electrician to come in and poke about with his screwdriver. As I returned home from work each evening for a week, I was forced to share what little space we had with this tradesman, while he tried to figure out what was wrong. My complaints to the owner naturally fell on deaf ears.

One evening, as we huddled in the cold living room, we were startled by the crash of breaking glass all around us. My God. What now? Were the windows falling in? No, not quite. But the pictures were beginning to fall off the walls. One very large and very cheap print lay in splinters beside us. Mercifully, it did not land on top of us. As we gathered up the shards of glass, my brain was already one step ahead. Write this down and send the information to the owner immediately, my mind told me. There was no way I was going to be paying for that when the time came for my deposit to be returned. This time, all bases would be covered.

As mentioned, the maisonette came with its own parking space directly under the trees outside our front door. Now our abode was No. 32, yet the number painted on the ground was No. 45. I had noticed this on day one and had enquired from the estate agent.

"Oh, don't worry about that," he assured me.

True, I had enough to think about without taking on minutiae like that. Big mistake.

Sometime during the months of October, I came out early one morning to find my car covered in a series of horrible slushy purple piles. Birds, I thought. What a horrible mess. So it was off to the car wash. However, the next morning the number of purple splodges had increased. What bothered me most was that two months earlier I had eventually taken my courage in my hands and traded in my rusty decaying old Mazda and bought myself a brand new Ford Ka, got on the 'Never Never'. I had been on the verge of investing in a used car, never having owned a brand new car before in my life. However, my daughter had intervened and argued that I deserved something nice in my life. Some little treat. I was not good at giving myself little treats.

Always save the money for the rainy day, had been my marital motto for twenty-eight years. Now, to my utter despair, my beautiful shiny black 'bubble car' was taking on the appearance of some monster from the deep every morning I opened my front door. What kind of birds were these, I wondered, or what kind of diet were they on? The 'stuff' that they were dumping on my car was impossible to remove. I could not afford to power jet the car every day.

Then one Saturday morning as I scrubbed away in despair, my neighbour came into the street.

"I see, you're having problems from the tree. Probably best not to park there," he volunteered.

He then went on to explain that the bird droppings were in fact huge soft berries from the overhanging branches of the tree. All of the previous occupants had the same problem. No one ever used that parking space. It did actually belong to No. 45, but they parked further away in what was actually my allocated space. I was livid. Zorba had purposely and knowingly tricked me. That afternoon, I parked my car in the spot allocated to 32, my number, and went back inside.

Two hours later, when I went to my car to go shopping, a pickup van was parked across my path, blocking my exit. Could it perhaps be the resident from No. 45? I knocked on their door. Instant regret. Six foot four, grimy vest, tattoos on biceps, and shaven head.

"Could you move your truck, please, Sir? I can't get my car out," I ventured, my body trembling more with each syllable.

"You're parked in my fucking spot! I've been in that spot for five years! Get your car out of there! Now!"

I stood my ground.

"But it says No. 32 on there," I ventured with more bravado than I felt inside.

"Mr Alcott and I have a deal," he replied politely at first. "Now get your car out of there, or do you want me to move it for you!"

He reached inside his door for his car keys, lunged towards his truck, climbed behind the wheel and glared at me as he reversed, leaving me space to remove my offending little Ford Ka. Meekly, I drove away, tears brimming in my eyes. When I got to the top of the road, the tears flowed. They flowed in rivers of frustration, desperation and fear. Fear that nothing in my life would ever go right for me. Fear that these troubles would lay ahead of me forever.

No home, no friends, no one to turn to in times like this. All I needed was someone to put their strong arms around me and say, "I will take care of you." I was just getting so tired of taking care of myself all the time. And as for Richard, no matter how much he wanted to be there for me, it wasn't practically possible.

For the months of December and January, the weather became so cold that Luke and I were forced to retire to bed at 6.30 pm each evening. The only place we had some heat was in the bedroom, and of course we had the electric blanket. The minute we got home from work after I had collected him from a friend's house, he climbed into bed while I fixed us something to eat, wearing my overcoat and warmed by a tiny electric wall heater in the kitchen and from the heat from the cooker. He would start his homework while I cooked. Then we huddled together in the double bed, ate our dinner and watched TV until 9 pm when it was time for sleep.

And still, the owner refused to do anything. Eventually, I had enough. I vowed I was going to get us a home of our own. I had no choice. My health was beginning to suffer and I was quickly loosing my sense of humour.

I approached a mortgage company and got an appointment for one Saturday morning. I knew I was going to have to lie, but I had little choice. The usual questions followed. Occupation? Husband's occupation? Income? Husband's income? Deposit available? Well, I answered all of these questions truthfully. The only part I left out was that my husband was not actually with me on this venture. After a quick tot of their figures, they joyfully informed me with beaming smiles on their faces that they could give us a 95 per cent mortgage, which would be in place by the following week.

Well, how could they refuse me after all? My husband had an income of well over £100,000 a year. He was a respectable medical doctor and a government minister. I had a respectable income, for a woman, or what they would refer to as 'a second income'. Where could they find a safer couple of clients than that? Trouble was, the big income was living on the other side of the Irish Sea leading a totally idyllic life. Not a care in the world. I suppose it showed the depth of my insanity or my desperation at that time. For two days I walked around on a cloud. I made appointments and viewed some beautiful houses and flats in nice areas, actually believing that in a few short weeks, my son and I were going to be living in one of them.

I drove to the Purley Way, lined with furniture shops, carpet shops, kitchen shops, curtain shops. I saw everything that I had ever wanted but had never been able to afford throughout my married life. I picked out the paint and the wallpaper. I saw myself being able to invite people over for dinner, instead of sitting on our own night after night, huddled together. But dreams must come to an end.

On Monday morning when I got a phone call at work from the mortgage company asking me when it would be suitable for my husband and I to come in to sign the relevant papers, I knew the game was up. What had I been thinking of? Had I been like a lost soul in the desert, gasping to find the mirage that never existed? There had never even been a realistic chance.

For weeks after this episode of insanity, I sunk into utter desolation. What was I going to do? There was no way out. My friends at home were full of suggestions.

"Come back," they said. "It won't be that bad."

But I knew that however bad my life in England was, going back to the situation I had fled in Donegal would be the equivalent of jumping into the fires of hell. I had to keep in the forefront of my mind the emotions I had felt on those last terrible days before I left. I could not run the risk of letting them go from my mind. If I did, then I knew that I would be in severe danger of convincing myself, as I had for years, that things would be okay or that people would change. I would believe that things would get better. I could not allow myself the luxury of letting go. Not yet. And so I resolved to fight on, forcing myself to believe that one day, we would be able to climb out of the mire that was South London.

My next plan of action was to withhold the rent on our flat. I knew this was risky, as I was reneging on my contract to pay seven hundred pounds per month for this hellhole. I had since discovered that the owner, the son of the acting owner, was actually in prison for non-payment of council tax. The withholding of the rent drove his mother into a frenzy and within two weeks, we had an eviction notice through our door. I was thrilled. At least we could get out of there. The deposit covered our last four weeks' rent. She even called me as a 'bloody nuisance' on the phone. I shook with fear and rage. I became terrified that she might turn up at the flat some evening with a couple of heavies, to keep me quiet.

A week after we moved out, she accused me of doing five hundred pounds worth of damage to her flat – that included fifty pounds for the cheap picture. A likely story. In fact, we were the ideal tenants, and left the place in a better state than we found it. She threatened to send debt collectors to my place of work, just to get money out of me. My boss was forced to alert Security if anyone inquired about the location of my office in the hospital. She left daily messages on my answering machine and rang my mobile phone on a continuous basis, with various threats to 'get me'. During this time, my health deteriorated and my blood pressure rose to a dangerously high level. My doctor advised me to take a week off work to deal with the stress. I reluctantly took just two days off. Sitting around in a hostile flat worrying about our future was not the answer. At least while working, I was too busy to think.

This time, however, I did not rush out and rent another flat. My wonderful daughter suggested that we once more come and stay at her place, even if it still meant sharing a room with the baby. However, they were in the throes of moving to a bigger house, so we knew the overcrowding was merely a temporary inconvenience. And, of course, it gave me a chance to look for alternative accommodation at my leisure. Thus began my association with storage companies, an association which gave me cause to use extremely unrepeatable language over the following months.

21

The Pen is Mightier...

In November 1999, just before I moved out of the third flat, an unusual and wonderful part of my life began to unfold. Little did I realise where it would lead me in the following years. Purely by chance, I started to write a column for the *Sunday Independent*. It all started quite by accident. A train accident, in fact. More precisely, the Paddington rail disaster in which up to thirty people tragically lost their lives.

I was working that day in the hospital nearby, when we were put on full alert to receive the injured. I sat at my computer after the rush had died down and penned my thoughts and observations on the day's event. Next morning, I faxed my copy to the *Sunday Independent*, and that was how it all began. One month later, they made me an offer I could not refuse – in the form of my own fortnightly column, and of course, money. I was broke and the thought of getting paid to do something I loved was just what I needed to boost my morale.

I had been writing for years, but never had the courage to submit anything for publication. I do recall, however, making copies of my very first book when I was six. I got some carbon paper from my father and made four copies. Then I industriously sewed the pages together with needle and thread, made covers for them, ironed them very flat, and gave them to my friends. An innocent childhood fairytale was the subject, if my mind serves me correctly, with perhaps a rosy view of the future.

As my column became more established, many people asked me why I continued to write about my private life every week. Some friends and family strongly disagreed with my decision. The truth was, I wrote for a variety of reasons. One was that I believed that if I wrote about my family, then it would save reporters making things up as they went along – most of it far from the truth.

However, one reason in particular was and still is the most important of all. Since 1999 I have received acres of correspondence from people I have never met, whose lives have been affected by many of the subjects I have written about. These included destructive relationships, abuse, both physical and psychological, alcoholism, separation, divorce, and domestic violence in general. It was gratifying to pick up a letter and see that my words and my experiences had brought solace to someone.

I never aspired to be anyone's agony aunt, but the truth is that there are thousands of lovely people out there who are desperately unhappy and isolated – undeservedly. They suffer daily at the hands of another, and just don't know what to do about it. They are powerless to stop the pain. This, I know.

So many times you hear that those who are unhappy have only themselves to blame. They may be looked upon as whingers.

"Pull yourself together and get on with life," they're told.

But for those who are trapped in abusive relationships, being on the receiving end of either physical or mental bullying, the solution unfortunately is not quite so simple.

Some years ago, I read an article in a newspaper, written by a woman, which left me feeling extremely angry indeed. This female journalist was suggesting that women in abusive relationships knowingly married abusive men. It was absolutely no one's fault, but their own. They should therefore just put up with their lot and not complain, or else get out. They should, she claimed, in an even more ridiculous sentence, tell the bully to stop.

"Oh, so that's how it's done," says the woman with the bruised ribs or the battered self-image.

"Okay. So when he comes home tonight, I'll just say 'John dear, I would like you not to shout at me or hit me any more'."

"Oh, I'm sorry, Mary dear. I thought you liked me shouting at you and abusing you. Yes, of course, I will stop now that you have asked me to."

What an easy solution. What a load of utter rubbish. On reading that article, I felt the anger boil up inside me. How could she possibly know? She obviously had no experience of the situation. I wanted to write to the newspaper concerned and voice my objections. But in those days, with my self-esteem at an all-time low, I just didn't have the confidence to air my views to anyone.

In recent years, I also received many letters from the wives of menopausal men. In other words, men who have suddenly realised that they are fast approaching, or have already reached, middle age. They fear that they have missed something, or God forbid, that they may be past whatever it is they are supposed to be missing in the first place. Gone past being an object of desire to the opposite sex, perhaps. I'm not referring to all men on this planet, just those with so little faith in themselves that they continuously need the admiration of others to make them feel like a real man. Whatever that is. These men plunder the earth, causing pain and heartache to those who love them. I read some of these letters with tears in my eyes, and I can feel the writer's pain.

"He has become so cold towards me."

"He treats me like I no longer exist."

"He doesn't even answer me when I speak to him."

"He stays out all night and won't tell me where he has been."

"He has started buying himself new boxer shorts and hiding all the old ones at the back of the wardrobe."

"I found an empty condom wrapper down the back of the mattress, when I came back from a weekend at my mother's."

Do men think women are stupid? Instinctively, a woman knows when her partner is being unfaithful. She knows that he is lying to her. She knows that she could in fact hire a private detective if she really wanted to. Yet somewhere deep inside, she doesn't really want to know the truth. If she can somehow convince herself that she is imagining it all, then everything will be okay. But will it? Will it not eat away inside her, turning her into a bitter and twisted human being? Will her only obsession in life be wondering who her husband is with when he's not at home? Will she be able to survive the continuous humiliation which he will bring to her life? Will she be able to ignore the sad sympathetic looks she gets from her neighbours?

Men get so stupid when they are having an affair, and this just compounds the hurt and pain they inflict. They make it so obvious, and yet think they are being so cunning. They don't seem to realise that women are a much more intuitive breed and can pick up subtle changes at a thousand paces. Who do they think they are fooling when they giggle into the phone like an adolescent schoolboy, speaking in hushed tones and absentmindedly shuffling their free hand down the front of their trousers?

When they say they are going to the shop for milk and come back two hours later empty handed, but wearing a smile akin to the proverbial cat that got the cream, so to speak, who are they kidding?

When they leave their credit card statements lying around on the kitchen table with strange amounts charged in strange restaurants, what are they thinking of? When the telephone bill arrives and there are eighty-five calls to one unfamiliar number in one month, isn't it being just a bit obvious? When that number is dialled and one hears the familiar female voice of a woman down the road answering, does this all add to the thrill of the deception? Is it perhaps another form of control?

"So what if she does find out?" he assures himself.

"She can't do anything to stop me."

"I can do what I want."

"She isn't going to leave because she has nowhere else to go."

"She has no money."

"And anyway, who else would have her?"

"No, I have her right where I want her, so I don't care. I'm just going to enjoy myself. To hell with her feelings."

Yes folks. It happens.

One of the best lessons I have learnt from writing for a major newspaper is how to accept criticism and rejection. Certainly, criticism is something that most of us have a problem with. It hurts us. I have learnt, however, that it is just another person's way of looking at things. On the whole, writing for a newspaper is a marvellous experience. It became my newfound joy because writing about my personal experiences was therapeutic. Nothing compares to picking up the paper on the morning of publication and reading one's own words in black and white. It is a part of my life I feel very lucky to have.

22

A House Divided

Newspapers may have been the path to my newfound joy, but nothing can prepare you for the shocks and blows they also deliver. Well, this time it was a bright sunny Sunday morning on 5 April 1998. I was up from Donegal and staying in a Dublin B&B for the weekend, while attending a training course in psychotherapy in Dun Laoghaire. I had thoroughly enjoyed what took place on the Saturday and was eagerly looking forward to more of the same on Sunday. At 7.30 am my mobile phone rang. It was my husband.

"There's something in the paper about me this morning. I thought I should let you know," he said.

"What sort of something?" I asked, not unduly worried.

He was in the habit of over-exaggerating things about himself.

"There's a photograph of me, and then another one of someone coming out of my flat," he went on.

"What sort of photograph?"

"Oh, it's just a photograph of Anne Doyle the newsreader, who's supposed to have been around at my flat one night."

"What are they saying about it?"

"Oh, they're trying to make something out of nothing. Saying that I was with her one night."

"And were you?" I asked innocently.

"Of course, I wasn't. What would I be doing with her? I hardly even know her. They're just trying to make something out of it, these damn newspapers."

"So how did they get all this then?"

"Oh, for God's sake, forget about all that. Look, if they ring you or try to get in touch with you, just say nothing. Do you hear me, just say absolutely nothing."

"Of course, I won't say anything. Don't worry about it," I reassured him. "I'm sure it'll all die down soon. I'll get the paper on my way to the course and talk to you after I've read it. Just don't worry."

I stopped to get petrol on the way to Dun Laoghaire and popped into a shop to get the paper and see what all the fuss was about. I looked on the shelf, trying to remember which paper he had said this 'little' article was in.

Then I felt the floor go from under me. He hadn't prepared me for what I was about to see – at all. There on the shelf, filling the front page was a photo of him and her and then underneath, one of me, the poor cheated wife with the sad hurt face. I thought I was going to pass out and only steadied myself with the aid of the shelf. This was no little piece hidden somewhere on page twenty-three. This was a national headline. I didn't know whether it was that or the sickening sight of him with another woman that hit me the biggest blow. Probably, the latter. It was as though my worst nightmare had materialised in front of me.

I managed to make my way back to my car and tried to read what was being said. But it didn't stop at the front page. Continued on page two, it said. And there we were. More photos. More 'facts' about our lives. More dirt dragged out for the world to see. I read about how devastated I was. It even informed me that I was separated from my husband. He was now my ex-husband. Well, that was big news to me.

For some unknown reason, I continued my journey and attended the second day of the course. All through the day, I felt in some sort of suspended state, looking down on the scene below like an observer. I couldn't seem to feel anything. In hindsight, I was obviously in total shock. My system had shut down to protect me.

At lunchtime, a group of us walked across the road to a shopping centre for lunch. I was terrified that someone would go into the newsagents at the entrance, and see my photograph. I would be found out. A fraud. An impostor. Guilty as sin. I would then be kicked off the course. I had actually done nothing to be ashamed of, yet I still felt that I was the guilty one. Force of habit, no doubt.

At about 5.30 pm that evening, when the course had come to an end, my guard dropped. I sat into my car and cried my eyes out. I was terrified, and the worst thing was, I didn't even know why. I was far from home and had no one to turn to. I rang my husband at his apartment somewhere in the vicinity of Dun Laoghaire and asked if I could come and see him. I needed someone to put their arms around me and tell me that I was safe. But he refused to let me anywhere near his apartment.

"I'm being watched," he hissed conspiratorially.

"Will you meet me someplace? Please."

"No. I don't want to be seen talking to you."

But what had I done? Six months earlier, things had come to a head. For over three years, my husband had not taken a day off work, had a break or had a holiday of any sort. He was persistently cranky and cross. I was concerned because he badly needed a break. Then I had a brainwave. From the sale of my late mother's house, I had got some money so I decided to put it to good use. I would give him a Christmas present fit for a king. After checking with his office in the Department of Tourism, and asking advice from various colleagues, I bought him a holiday.

Skiing for a week in Andorra, shortly after Christmas Day – my husband, myself and our little boy. The Dáil would be closed down, departmental offices on holidays, and there would be no reason in the world for him not to take a well-deserved break. Everyone thought it was a brilliant idea.

It was all booked and paid for, and I was intending to present it as a surprise to both my husband and son on Christmas morning. However, one of my older sons was not too sure of how his father might react to the news, and hinted strongly at the surprise, two weeks early.

My husband was aghast. He was angry. He was furious. He was adamant that he would not be going anywhere with us. One week before Christmas, he told me to cancel the entire trip. He even went so far as accusing me directly of trying to undermine his career, by forcing him out of the country, enabling others to usurp his position. He accused me of trying to make him feel guilty for letting down our young son.

This was the last straw for me. In a final effort at keeping my life together, I pleaded with my husband to move out of our house and to live somewhere else until such time as he could see his way to treating me as a human being. His response was to suggest building a wall through the centre of the house, with each of us living on either side. That was too much and I told him so.

He finally agreed to leave, and while my son and I were on our skiing trip, he moved his belongings into a rented house just around the corner. At least there, he could come and go as he pleased. But over the next three months, he was never out of our house. He would come in, make himself a cup of coffee, and sit down watching TV with his feet on the coffee table. He didn't seem to know what he wanted. One week before the 'Doyle' saga, I had invited him for dinner and he and my son had sat and watched *Match of the Day* together. We had been getting on fine.

However, that night in Dublin when I needed him, he refused to see me. I was devastated. I drove back to Donegal the following morning in a daze. As I neared home, I was dreadfully afraid of reporters and photographers being parked at my front door. The story had not died down with the Sunday papers. Instead, it was carried in all the Monday tabloids. I had been warned not to speak to anyone.

That Monday afternoon, a knock at my door came from two local high-ranking Fianna Fáil men. They sat with me in the living room for four hours, as I thought, consoling me and offering me support. I was later to discover that they had actually been sent to keep an eye on me. To make sure that I did not speak to reporters about my husband. Perhaps they were afraid I would say, "Oh yes. This has happened before. He has had loads of affairs before this."

In my foolishness that day I actually thought they cared about me. But, I should have known. They were there to protect the Minister. In the ensuing weeks, my life became unbearable. My husband blamed me for the entire newspaper debacle. It was all my fault.

"Can you imagine how poor Anne Doyle is feeling, being dragged into all of this? Can you imagine how embarrassing this is for her, instead of selfishly thinking about yourself all the time?

"This could ruin my career," he continued accusingly.

Was I really going mad? What had I done? Why was I to blame? Had I done something terrible that I didn't know about? It was all very confusing. My older children were being dragged into it from all sides. When I left the house to go shopping, I knew that everyone was looking at me. I could not go back to my job. I felt like I was walking the streets naked. If someone spoke to me in the supermarket, I jumped out of my skin. I trusted no one or nothing, except one true friend. Some people said, "Don't worry about it. Everyone will have forgotten all about it by next week." Wonderful consolation. When would I be able to forget? Maybe never.

Lots of political people called to the house. I thought they were my friends. I was wrong again, I was to soon discover. When push came to shove, they jumped to the side of political power. I suppose one cannot blame them really. What power did I have to get jobs for their sons, to get grants for their businesses, to get promotions for their brothers-in-law? None at all. Meanwhile, week after week, the verbal and mental abuse got worse.

Finally, I went away for a weekend in early May. I arrived back on Sunday afternoon to find my husband spreadeagled in the back garden of my home, sunbathing in his boxer shorts. He did not seem to know where he lived. He didn't want me. He didn't want to have anything to do with our marriage, yet he was never out of my hair.

No, Anne Doyle did not drive me out of my home. She was merely number ten or n on the list. Just another notch on the bedpost, so to speak.

23

End of an Era

*A*s 1999 drew to a close, deciding where to spend Christmas and ring in the new millennium filled my mind. Despite reservations about my ability to face going back to Donegal and all the ghosts it held for me, I decided shortly before Christmas to return for a brief visit, after an absence of eighteen months. The memory of that fateful date in May 1998, when I had left hurt, crying and terrified of what lay ahead, was still with me. But I knew I had made the right decision. At the time, I just had to get out at all costs.

It was with mixed emotions that I faced the journey. Now I was arriving back, after what seemed to me like years, not knowing how I was going to feel or how I was going to cope. Fortunately, this time my daughter, her husband and my grandson were with me on the journey, driving from London to Fishguard, and then Rosslare to Dublin and eventually on to Donegal. It was a very gradual transition back onto Irish soil rather than flying directly to Belfast or Derry as I had done in the past when visiting my daughter in London. The longer, slower journey gave me more time to acclimatise.

One of the things that surprised me after being out of the country for so long was the difference in the Irish landscape, compared to England. I sound like a 'stage' Irish emigrant when I say that I had forgotten how rural the whole place was. Driving up from Wexford, I was more aware than previously of the number of small towns, and the solitary huge new houses built in the middle of nowhere. Secret lottery winners people used to say! And the state of the roads – the potholes hadn't changed!

Having left London at 6 am that morning, we stayed overnight in a well-known establishment in Dublin. Immediately, we were shocked by the exorbitant prices. My son-in-law offered to bring drinks to our room from the bar before we retired for the night. Yet he was immediately relieved of ten pounds for one coke, one sparkling water and one pint of beer. Very much over the top, we thought.

However, next morning, we stopped for breakfast at a popular hotel on the outskirts of Castleblaney en route. There we ordered three full Irish breakfasts. Quick as a flash, we had a great big pot of strong tea in front of us, with a large plate of toast in its wake. Five minutes later, three plates of freshly grilled bacon and expertly fried eggs, totally grease-free, arrived. I had never appreciated good Irish bacon so much in my life. Though normally not a big breakfast person, I truly enjoyed this delicious meal. Not a scrap of food remained on our plates. And overall, a much better image that Ireland needed to convey to its tourists, we thought.

As we came closer to Donegal, my stomach began to lurch. I was not quite sure what to expect. One part of me was dying to see all my friends again after such a long absence. Another part was fretting about how I would feel when I saw my home. I had put so much of myself into that house when we built it five years earlier, wanting to leave some sort of legacy to my children when the time came. It was also the home I had hoped my children and grandchildren would come back to for visits. Now *I* was coming back as a visitor.

My husband was not in favour of me coming back for Christmas, but my children had been adamant that they wanted the family together for the start of the new millennium, and he had relented. How was I going to cope with meeting this man I had not seen for almost two years? I was terrified. I had been forced to try and forget him. Would all my old feelings for him come to life again? Had they ever died?

It had been the great problem in my relationship with Richard. I was still in love with my husband. Was there a difference between being 'in love' and 'loving' someone, I wondered. Whichever, I just couldn't get my husband out of my mind. Certain aspects of his image had begun to grow dim, and I panicked. I could not remember, for instance, the colour of his ties or the feel of the fabric in his suits, or the shape of his face. I was terrified to let go. For over thirty years I had seen this man practically every day of my life. Now, it was so long since I had set eyes on him. Through my own decision, I had refused all offers from friends to forward me the local papers through the post. I knew his picture would be all over them.

I had decided against speaking to him on the phone for the first four months of my time in London, but as the months progressed I had begun to ring him at his office in Dublin, or at home in our house. Each time I came off the phone I was upset or in tears.

"Why do I keep phoning him?" I asked myself.

Then slowly I realised what was happening. I was suffering from withdrawal symptoms. I had lived with verbal and mental abuse for so long, to the extent that it had become an integral part of my life. Maybe it had provided me with some sort of weird identity or even some misguided notion that I provided a service by being his verbal punch bag. That I was actually useful for something in this life. However, now that I didn't have it every day, I had lost my usefulness. It was like coming off heroin. I needed my daily fix. Some times I rang his office in the Department of Tourism only to be told he wasn't available to speak to me.

"Oh no, Mrs McDaid. The Minister isn't here today, he's in America until the 14th."

Or "He has been in Egypt all week and won't be back till Monday."

Every time, it was a different country. These messages from his office tore into my heart like a red-hot knife. Each time I cried with frustration and hurt. But, I still loved him. Always in the back of my mind was the thought that if he ever found out that I was seeing another man, there would be no hope of us getting back together again. Something I had always hoped for, no matter what I told my friends and family.

Therefore I had to remain unattached, so to speak. Although why, I do not know. It was no secret that he had already been through more women both in Dublin and Donegal than I could bring myself to think about. Indeed very little attempt was made to hide most of them. I could forgive him, for some odd reason, but I doubted if he would ever forgive me. So I had to be extremely careful. I was stuck solidly on the fence though life was rushing hurriedly by.

And yet, I wonder to this day if things would have turned out differently had I been standing on Platform 12 at Victoria just one year earlier, when Richard was unattached and still looking to share his life with someone.

Fortunately that Christmas, things worked out much better than any of us had expected. On our arrival, my husband was on hand to greet us, along with Luke who had flown over from London a week earlier. The house was decorated for Christmas, with the fires lighting and the tree lights beckoning in the window. I took it all very gradually at first, spending the first hour just getting used to the living room, and not moving any further. I felt slightly like an invited guest, not quite sure of my role. Should I make a cup of tea myself or should I wait to be asked? It was weird. Eventually, I was able to move on to the kitchen and the music room, where my piano was waiting.

It was some hours before I had the courage to go upstairs to my bedroom. Here, I found everything just as I had left it. Nothing had changed. Nothing had moved. Everything was in its place on my dressing table. My dressing gown lay over the back of the chair, just as I had left it. My clothes were still hanging in the wardrobe. I had taken just the bare essential summer clothes with me when I fled. The calendar on the wall in the kitchen remained at May 1998. Part of me felt like I had just been away overnight. Another part felt that I had died on that day. I felt like I was living in someone else's body.

Once the word got around that I was back, my friends began calling and we arranged lots of meetings. Unfortunately, I missed out on seeing many good friends, simply through lack of hours in the day. Since I had left, the town of Letterkenny had been transformed into the metropolis of the northwest. As I drove through the main street with my daughter on Christmas Eve, I could not comprehend the number of old landmarks that had disappeared and been replaced by new buildings. At last, they had a new state-of-the-art theatre. I thought of all the children's musical productions that I'd been involved in over the years and the abysmal and inadequate conditions we'd worked under. It was wonderful to know that in the future the children and their mentors would hopefully have the best of stages on which to display their talents.

Also, I noted that the number of new restaurants and hotels had mushroomed. They were everywhere. I managed to sample a few of them during my visit, surprised only at the high cost of the food in comparison to London prices. However, having a choice of places to enjoy good food, good wine and good friends was encouraging. Never again would the tourists have any cause to complain about the lack of facilities in Donegal!

Christmas Day was a wonderfully peaceful family day, just what we all needed after the chaos of the past years. After Mass, it was lovely to stand outside the church and meet old acquaintances again, all of whom welcomed me back warmly. It made me feel very privileged.

Leading up to Christmas I had been very aware that my grandson did not know what was going on, due to his deafness. Then on Christmas Eve, I mentioned to a friend that I wished to get hold of a Santa Claus costume, so that one of the menfolk could play Santa on Christmas morning, especially for Cameron's benefit. Wonderful friend that she is, she immediately sorted me out. Early on Christmas morning, complete with white beard and wig, red suit, boots and bell, my eldest son arrived at the house bearing a sack of gifts for everyone. The look on Cameron's face made it all worthwhile. Hopefully, it will be a memory that will stay with him for years to come.

New Year's Eve of the millennium was a night that left many people not knowing where to go because of severe overpricing. But still it was a night to remember. We decided on a big family party at home, with daughter, sons, brothers, sisters, nieces, nephews, boyfriends, girlfriends, mother-in-law, numerous in-laws and also some close friends and their children. It was lovely to celebrate the millennium with four generations from my mother-in-law down to my little grandson and every age in between. At midnight, over thirty of us happily counted in the New Year together. Unfortunately, my husband opted to spend the night in Dublin.

All too soon, it was time to go away again. But this time, I was ready to go. My spirits had been boosted by seeing all my old friends again.

"Will you be staying now that you have summoned up the courage to come back?" people asked, on first meeting me again.

"No!" I would answer emphatically.

I could not come back to stay now. I had managed to move on to a more peaceful and structured way of life. True, I had to work much harder and for much longer hours than ever before, but I also had more control over my own state of mind. The behaviour and moods of my husband could no longer buffet me. I could get up in the morning feeling good, and manage to feel good right through the day if I made a conscious decision.

For many years I had walked around Letterkenny with my head down. I was so convinced that I was a bad and terrible person, that I could not look people in the eye, or speak to them. This naturally gave the impression that I was a snob, while secretly inside I saw myself as unworthy of people's company.

Now at last, I could walk down the street with my head held high, speaking to everyone that I met, and being genuinely friendly. Here at last was the real me – a kind and caring friend. I was sleeping more peacefully, without the aid of medication and no longer suffered from intense headaches and a churning anxiety in my stomach. In all, I was leading a more stress-free life. It was difficult to imagine London being less stressful than Donegal, but in London, perhaps I had more physical anxiety, but I had far less mental and emotional stress.

I now felt good about myself and for that reason I couldn't take the chance of returning to the negative feelings forced on me when I left. Perhaps, in time to come, when things might be different, I would reconsider it. But as it stood then, there was no place for me in Donegal.

24

Gung-ho Politicos

As any TD or their spouse will tell you, there's nothing like a little junket to spice up your life. From the spouse's point of view, it is certainly one of the few rewards to be gained from the job. Naturally, there has to be some spin-offs to such political domination of our lives. All my life, I had longed to travel, to experience new continents, new cultures, new lifestyles. From the time I was a small child, I would spend hours dreaming about visiting India, where I had a pen pal; America, where my aunts lived; and China, where the music was enchanting.

In the first three or four years of my husband's political career, he allowed me to push myself on to a couple of junkets. I use the word push unreservedly, as I travelled on these trips unwelcomed. In other words, my husband would have preferred to travel without me. However, I held my ground and bought my ticket. Yes, a political spouse must always pay for his or her own plane ticket. I'm not sure if that applies to ministerial junkets, as I was 'sacked' before any of these came about.

My introduction to the political junket came in 1990. The prospect of three days in Brussels had me jumping up and down with excitement. I discovered then that government travel was the only way to go. Certainly the group of Fianna Fáil, Fine Gael and Labour TDs on the trip was treated like royalty in the VIP lounge at Dublin Airport. There was a free bar and nibbles, comfortable couches, and free newspapers and magazines. Then a VIP exit to the aircraft – none of your pushing and shoving with the common man – followed by first-class seats in the front row. We had champagne for breakfast and real knives and forks and no plastic glasses. And just as the door was about to close, Ray McSharry was spirited aboard – an EU Commissioner on a connecting flight from Sligo to Brussels!

On arrival in Brussels, we were collected from the aircraft by limousine and whisked to our five-star hotel, naturally. The political itinerary included a session in the European Parliament, at which some of our group were due to speak. But what was I to do? Well, a very special Dublin woman made the trip extremely comfortable for me. Monica Barnes, the former Fine Gael TD, has always been a wonderfully caring person.

"Marguerite, you just keep following me until someone stops you," she advised.

I did as I was told and walked past guards, officials, security doors, and ten minutes later, I was sitting next to the British MP, Edwina Currie – of the egg fame – as she addressed the assembly. I spent a most enjoyable and educational two hours with my headphones on, listening to the various foreign languages and observing the translators in their booths, switching from one lingo to another without batting an eyelid. The day was finished off by a hilarious night out on the town with the inimitable Mark Killilea, the MEP from Galway at the time.

Two years later, I was off on the trail once more. This time, our destination was Denmark, and we were going for five days. It was getting better. There was no excuse for me not being taken along this time, as everyone else's spouse was going. As it transpired, those five days compensated for all the laughter I had been denied during the previous ten years. The combination of one previous Minister for Justice, in the form of Seán Doherty from Roscommon, and a witty Corkman in the form of Ned O'Keefe, along with a few other characters, made for one complete howl from beginning to end.

The purpose of our visit was never absolutely clear, but I do believe it had something to do with learning how to raise veal calves under dubious conditions. Another reason was learning how to manage giant refuse problems, a matter the Danes had down to a fine art. A visit to a spotlessly clean pig farm had also been on the agenda.

It also became necessary for us to visit the headquarters of the Heineken brewery, where it would have been unstatesmanlike not to have sampled the various beers offered. The highlight of our trip, however, was a dinner in our honour at the Danish Government buildings in Copenhagen. Could Leinster House ever match that, I wondered? This was dining at its finest. The amount of silverware and gold-trimmed glassware for each table setting equalled that of Buckingham Palace. The choice of wine with each course was excellent – everything down to the most wonderful dessert wine ever to grace my palate.

The company was superb and I was seated next to a high-ranking Danish official who filled me in on the national attitude to birth control. One or two children per couple was the general rule. Anything above that was considered breeding like rabbits. Abortion was seen in the same acceptable light as going to the dentist. Possibly one or two visits needed per year, depending on age. On learning that many of us seated around the table were parents to maybe six or seven children, if not more in certain cases, the Danish official inquired as to the reason. I duly informed him that it must be the weather!

Mr Doherty, being the senior politician in our midst, was called upon to say the *cúpla focail* that evening. Afterwards over a drink or six back at our hotel, he recounted a tale of a comrade caught in a similar position in China some years earlier. At a lavish reception one evening, the guest of honour was a well-respected Senior Cabinet Minister – the SCM. There ensued the usual round of speeches from the Chinese, both in English and in their mother tongue. Just seconds before our beloved SCM was due to speak, the Chinese dignitaries beseeched him to say a few words in his native Gaeilge.

Now the only words this poor man knew were *Tá* and *Níl*, both of which he had learnt from his party whip, as a raw young backbencher. Each long dreary day, as the division bell tolled in Leinster House, he had been obliged to enter the Dáil chamber and make his way through the relevant voting gate as instructed. Either *Tá* or *Níl*.

Undaunted by the task set to him by the Chinese, however, and in the style of the true political giant, he approached the microphone, pulled himself up to his full height, cleared his throat and began.

"*Ár n'Athair atá ar neamh, go naofar d'ainm, go dtagadh do ríocht...*" and so on and so on, until he had recited The Lord's Prayer in full. He even managed to include some meaningful pauses, and succeeded in pulling up just short of the final Amen. Well, that might have given the game away. Without further ado, he continued by way of translation.

"Ladies and Gentlemen, it is indeed an honour for me to be here this evening..." and proceeded with the translation.

As he retook his seat amid tremendous applause, he silently thanked old Sister Sheila who had all those years earlier drummed the Our Father and Hail Mary into his little head in a freezing schoolroom in the depths of rural Ireland. We gave him full marks for improvisation.

Then someone else recounted the story about the Cowboys and Indians. Rural by-elections used to be great fun, so I'm told, way back in those halcyon days before politicians lost some of the people's respect. In the final week before polling day, every TD and SCM would flock to some tiny hamlet, leaving the cares of the day behind in Dublin or in their own constituency. Long happy hours would be spent doorstepping innocent inhabitants, and blowing their own political trumpets to those unfortunate enough to be within earshot. After a hard day on the hustings, these workers would be quite thirsty. So it was off to the local for maybe a pint of two, or God forbid, on rare occasions maybe even a small Jameson.

The custom at the time was that the sitting TD, whose seat was secure, would often accommodate some of his colleagues in his own home overnight. On one such occasion, the colleague happened to be an SCM, and the TD's home was situated far out in the remote countryside. Around this period in our history, it was felt that some SCMs, particularly those in Justice and Defence, needed that little bit of extra security. To provide this, a mini arsenal of Garda weaponry was close to hand at all times, in the boot of the state car.

On the night in question, or rather early morning, as the party of revellers returned from the local in hilarious form and itching for the bit of craic, someone suggested a game of Cowboys and Indians. Well, boys will be boys, and very soon some well-armed politicos were doing their impression of The Lone Ranger, dashing about the adjoining field with whoops of joy, guns to the ready. I'm not sure which of them actually had the Kalashnikov, but I was assured it was in safe hands!

My third and final experience on the junket circuit was not an enjoyable one. In fact, it showed me very clearly just how some politicians and their families can abuse the power bestowed on them by the electorate. This time there was no jolly group, no Monica Barnes, but just two couples. I had a bad feeling from the outset, as my husband had put up a greater fight than ever to prevent me from going. But once again I held my ground. This time, the Asian continent was one that I had always wanted to visit since I was a child. I managed to borrow the money for my plane fare, so no one was going to stop me. One week later, I was sorry I had ever bothered.

Various incidents contributed to my disappointment. During one conversation over a drink, our travelling companions boasted that they sent four thousand Christmas cards to constituents each year. They didn't have to do anything to achieve this feat. A group of people did all the signing and enveloping each year for them. At approximately two people per house, that was eight thousand votes each time round. And, of course, pre-paid government envelopes cost nothing.

On a short flight to an adjoining country, there was another dissatisfying incident. We were travelling as envoys of the Irish Government, meeting members of other governments and indeed it would have been extremely important that we portray ourselves as such. However, on this particular transfer, the other politician opted to travel in shorts, tee shirt and runners minus his socks. Not a pretty sight on the Irish male in mid-January, I might add. His wife had opted for similar garb, while my husband and I had stuck to more conventional dress.

At the passport and visa control checkpoint, our comrade was asked for ID.

"We are members of the Irish Government," he retorted haughtily, giving the friendly guard a withering look.

As the surrounding officials cast dubious glances at this couple and their totally ungovernmental attire, comrade TD and his wife proceeded to let the officials know just what they thought of them. Their use of political power only left them looking foolish, I felt. If one wishes to receive respect, then show respect, is my motto. And above all, present yourself in a respectable manner. Shakespeare's word sprang to mind as I observed the distasteful spectacle before me, *Rich, not gaudy, for the apparel oft proclaimeth the man.*

Would ministerial junkets have been any better? It had all seemed so promising on that wonderful day in July 1997, when James was handed the ministerial portfolio of Tourism. It was beyond all our wildest dreams and aspirations. Ten minutes after his appointment was announced, the wives of other long-term ministers surrounded me, congratulating me on my good fortune.

"The first thing you must do tomorrow is find yourself a good childminder and a housekeeper," they suggested.

"This is *your* opportunity as well," they added. "This is where you can make up for all those long, lonely days and nights you've spend on your own, bringing up your children alone, while he goes to meetings and funerals, and is in Dublin all week. This is your reward."

At the time, I did not fully understand what they were saying.

"You be ready to go with him at the drop of a hat," they advised. "There'll be loads of foreign travel. There'll be loads of formal functions in Dublin. There'll be loads of entertaining, so go and get yourself a new wardrobe and be ready for everything. You'll have a brilliant time, and enjoy every minute of it, because it could be snatched away again as quickly as it arrived."

"The Tourism ministry is brilliant for travel abroad. You make sure you go on every trip," the wife of a past incumbent similarly advised me.

So was my childhood dream about to turn to reality? Was my burning desire to see the world and explore new cultures about to be sated? Was God smiling on me at last? Was I at last going to be able to spend time with my husband?

Sadly, no. None of this came to pass. After the initial excitement and celebration had died down somewhat, I got the opportunity to speak to him in the week following his appointment. It was at his plush office in the Department of Tourism.

"Can we make some plans now about our new lifestyle?" I asked.

"What about living arrangements in Dublin?" I continued. "Are you going to still share the house in Dublin?"

He looked at me in utter disbelief. Over the next thirty minutes, he took my dreams, my hopes, and my joy and ground them into the floor beneath his feet. His words rang in my ears.

"You can forget any crazy ideas you have about going anywhere with me," he declared. "You won't be attending any functions with me. And you certainly won't be travelling anywhere with me either.

"In fact, don't show your face around Dublin under any circumstance."

With regard to his living arrangements in Dublin, he duly informed me that he had already chosen a flat, the location of which would be kept secret from me. I would not be allowed to visit, whatsoever. My job was to remain in Donegal, run his house, look after our young son, and keep the constituency ticking over, as he put it. He would return to our home in Donegal periodically whenever his job took him there. This new post was his, and his alone. I had done nothing to help him reach this position in his life.

This left me gutted. Had he forgotten everything? Had he forgotten that it was left to me to choose and buy every item of his clothing since the day we were married? Every smart suit and every eye-catching tie.

Had he forgotten that it was I who transformed him into the best-groomed politician in Leinster House – as voted by his peers? Had he forgotten all the times I dragged him back from the gutter and poured coffee into him, lest he be found out by his peers? Had he forgotten the times that I literally had to sit on top of him to prevent him making a total fool of himself in public? Had he forgotten that it was I who wrote his speeches on the way to functions all over Donegal, when he was too tired or too hung over to think?

Yes, it seems he had. There was no place in his life for me at all. That he made crystally clear.

25

Couch Heaven

*I*t was now nearly two years since I had arrived in London and, eventually, my children had managed to convince their father that I needed to buy somewhere more permanent for us to live. It upset us every time we had to move from one grotty flat to another. He agreed to be guarantor for me to get a mortgage, on the understanding that I would sign a document stating that I would not renege on the loan repayments.

The thought of owning a property actually terrified me. What if I could not make the mortgage repayments? What if there was a slump in the property market and I was forced to sell up at well below my original buying price? I dreaded the thought that negative equity, which had affected thousands of homeowners in the early nineties in Britain, would happen to me too. Again, the fear of being put in prison in Britain reared its ugly head.

Anyway, I had to find someplace that I could afford. So the search was on again and I was back in the land of estate agents. But there were hundreds and thousands of houses for sale, they assured me. No problem there, but as for price – way beyond my budget. No harm in looking, I thought. In reality all that I could afford was a small two-bedroomed terrace house in a side street off the main London to Brighton road, which was fine to be getting on with. At least it would be ours and no one could tell us what we could or could not do inside our own four walls. But as with everything else in Britain, nothing was straightforward and simple.

Buying a house in Donegal was child's play compared to this. I should know, I had bought three of them over a period of twenty-five years. I was well accustomed to dealing with solicitors, surveyors, estate agents and builders. But nothing could have prepared me for the circus that followed. Initially, I was told that we should be able to complete the deal in six weeks. Three months later, we were still sharing the room with my daughter's baby. I thought at one stage that we were almost there, but then, my surveyor discovered rising damp in the living room wall of the property I was buying.

What should I do? Pull out and start all over again from the beginning. Take a risk and go ahead, hoping that the damp would not rise too high during my lifetime. I sought the advice of solicitor, bank manager, surveyor, builder and everyone else who knew anything about bricks and mortar. Each one had different advice to offer.

"I wouldn't touch it with a barge pole."

"A bit of damp will do no harm."

"The house is too old. Stay clear of it."

"Well, you're bound to get a bit of damp in a house that's over 100 years. Don't worry about it."

In the end, I made up my own mind. I persuaded the vendor to drop his price by the same amount it would cost to have the damp treated. I was taking a chance, but the truth was, I just couldn't go on any longer and the thought of starting from scratch again was more than I could take.

One Saturday morning towards the end of March 2000, I was handed the keys of our new home in the estate agent's office. I was trembling with excitement. We could move in that day. Thirty minutes later, however, I was trembling with rage. The pigs. The mess the previous owners had left behind was unforgivable. Six weeks earlier, my daughter and her husband had moved house and I had helped them. The immaculate condition in which they left their old house and the condition in which they found their new one was a joy to behold.

Cupboards cleaned, carpets vacuumed, bathroom sparkling – everything in order.

For some reason, I had expected the same. No such luck. The owners had even left a dish of cat food on the kitchen floor. The bedroom and living-room carpets had looked fairly okay when I had gone to view the house. But once the furniture was removed, I knew that I could not live in such dirt and dust. I doubted if they had cleaned the place since they purchased it four years earlier. The kitchen and bathroom were filthy. I had been looking forward to that day for so long, and it was just another nightmare. There was no way we could move in until I did some drastic overhauling.

First, I had to dash to the carpet shop to order some replacement floor covering. Thankfully, they had a cancellation and could deliver the following week. So far so good.

"Will you take away the old carpets?" I inquired innocently.

"Oh no, Madam. The room must be clear when our fitters arrive. All old covering must be disposed of and any furniture removed."

Back to the house and the remainder of my weekend was spent cutting up filthy, dusty, heavy old carpets into manageable-sized pieces, to be carried in the back of my Ford Ka to the local dump. I was on the verge of collapse after that. Eventually, the new floor covering was laid and it was time to get our bits and pieces installed. At this stage, our belongings were stored in a local warehouse, apart from any clothes needed at that time of year. Everything else had to be hauled out and transported again in the Ka. Not the most efficient vehicle for moving house perhaps, but the fifty trips backwards and forwards were a doddle. Well after all, I had been used to doing it all my life. Each of the fifteen times we had moved house in Ireland, it had been left to me to do the humping and the hauling. I knew no other way, unfortunately.

There was one other slight problem, however. It was impossible to buy furniture off the shelf, so to speak, in London. There was a ten- to twelve-week wait for everything – beds, tables, chairs, sofas, etc. To counteract that problem and because we could not afford 'proper furniture', we resorted to the land of flat packs, MFI and B&Q to be exact. Everything but the couch came with a list of assembly instructions.

The next three weeks were spent with screwdriver and hammer, as I assembled the kitchen table and four chairs, the wardrobes, the dressing table, my son's shelving unit, the coffee table and the TV stand. I did manage to buy a mattress off the peg, and for the first eight weeks, we slept on this on the bedroom floor. And for three months, we sat on pillows in the living room.

Then in July came the great day when the couch arrived. Disaster struck. The deliverymen couldn't get it turned in the narrow hallway to get it in through the living-room door. It was stuck. So they had to take it back to the warehouse, and a new one was ordered in its place and naturally, this one took another three months. To ease my aching back in the meantime I purchased a self assembly easy chair. At least it got me up off the floor for a few hours. The following week, they did deliver the beds, which I was able to screw together without too much difficulty. But the autumn leaves were falling before we managed to discard our pillows on the living-room floor for the comfort of our new couch. The amount of pleasure I got from that one new piece of furniture was amazing. In the meantime, I had painted most of the house and put some of my pictures on the walls, so it was really beginning to feel like home. Yes, home. Maybe now, we could be at peace.

26

At The Races

For the first two years that I was away from Ireland, my mind kept drifting back to what I thought I was missing at home. It seemed that every month there was something else to think back on. I couldn't get rid of the memories that were haunting me. The last week in July was a typical example. The Galway Races. The biggest festival in the West.

It all started for me in the mid-fifties. I had been weaned on the Galway Races. The three most important dates on the calendar of my young life: Christmas, my birthday and 'The Races'. Each year without fail, my father piled us into his trusty black Ford and off we went on our family pilgrimage to the Galway Races. The dodgems, the swing boats, the picnic, with the biggest treat of all yet to come. Yes, pink and white marble cake, washed down by fizzy bottles of lemonade in Lawlor's giant white tent beside the tote. What a treat! And the sun was shining, naturally.

I still remember the shouts.

"Race cards. Race cards. Cards a shillin', race cards."

The women and children from Dublin's Moore Street had decamped to Ballybrit in droves.

"Come and get me luvly bananas. Luvly ripe bananas. Two bob the lot, Mister." My father was in generous mood and our taste buds quivered as he handed over the money. All this excitement and we hadn't even got out of the car yet!

For the big races, the Plate and the Hurdle, we took up our vantage point behind the tall white rails on the final bend, half a furlong out from home. There was little to beat the excitement as the ground vibrated under our feet. Thirty or more giant packages of powerful horseflesh thundered past just inches from our noses, the colours of the jockeys' silks flashing in the brilliant sunlight. We cheered wildly for my father's horse.

"I can't see, Daddy, I can't see," I whimpered, and seconds later was hoisted onto his strong shoulders. And the sun was still shining.

In my early twenties, the Galway Races took on a new meaning. By then, Galway City had begun crawling out into the countryside, with factories and housing estates springing up within view of Ballybrit. This time, with my husband and college friends, our first point of call on passing through the turnstiles was the well-known 'long bar' under the main grandstand. It was here with a glass in one hand, and race card in the other that we got down to the extremely serious task of picking winners. Some of us relied on the old 'stick a pin method', while others close to my heart used the more scientific route, analysing handicap, weight, form, etc. Both methods proved quite successful in their own right, 'pins' possibly gaining a slight upper hand over equine science.

"Luck, pure luck," my beloved grumbled, as my selected chestnut No. 8 with Tommy Carberry astride galloped past the winning post ahead of the field, with my 2/6 on his nose.

And so the days and years progressed. Three days racing developed into six at Ballybrit. Serious betting, serious money and serious drinking became the order of the day and the week. For some an innocent fiver on the tote had turned into the more serious stuff with Terry Rogers *et al.* I was still getting the same pleasure and excitement from my one pound each way on an outsider.

Then as soon as the last race finished, it was a mad dash back to the city. There the pubs were waiting for us with open arms, and we were allowed to drink in peace well into the small hours. This was all thoroughly enjoyable for a few years, but good things rarely last. The sun no longer shone quite so brightly and pleasure was thin on the ground. There was no place in the bars of Ballybrit for our children, and strong paternal shoulders were otherwise occupied.

Somewhere along the way, I began to yearn for the uncomplicated simplicity and enjoyment of racing with my father, but sadly by then he was surely enjoying himself in heaven. Gradually as the years went by, the great festival became a form of self-flagellation, an event to be definitely avoided. The sunshine became but a distant memory.

During the 1980s and 1990s, I made a few visits with my husband, none very enjoyable. In August 1997 I attended Ballybrit for Ladies Day. I treated myself to a new outfit and even bought myself a fancy hat. By then, rows of expensive houses overlooked the starting gates opposite the stands, and the serious punters arrived by helicopter. Two weeks earlier I had asked my husband if I should book a hotel in the city for us. He was now Minister for Tourism and Sport and off the booze. On other occasions in the past, we had stayed with my mother, but with her death the previous October, I had no desire to return to her house. The memories would have been too painful. My husband argued that he possibly wouldn't attend the race meeting that year. Certainly he had no intention of booking into a hotel and being plagued by hangers-on for a week. If he did decide to go at all, he would stay with my sister. The previous three years, all his colleagues had booked rooms in the surrounding hotels and their wives had a brilliant week together. I missed out on all of that, staying at my mother's.

Eventually, I decided to attend Ladies Day accompanied by Luke and one of my older sons. After we arrived, I heard that my husband was in fact at the Races, hosting lunch in a corporate tent. After a while, my sons headed off to have their own fun, their spirits undampened by the heavy rain. Soon it came down in monsoon torrents so I decided to seek my husband out in the tent just before the first race. Security on the door was strict and I was not allowed in. My husband had to come out to see what I wanted. Eventually, he was embarrassed into inviting me to join the lunch he was hosting in the sumptuous surroundings. A space was made for me at the table, and his guests and their spouses were extremely friendly and welcoming. My husband glared at me from across the table. He was seething with rage. I was quivering with embarrassment inside, but dared not let my feelings show. However, the corporate hospitality was at its very best.

"Good afternoon, Minister. Good afternoon, Madam. Can I offer you a glass of champagne? We hope you have a pleasant day's racing." This was Fianna Fáil hospitality that money could not buy.

To all and sundry, I was having a brilliant time. I knew, however, that I would suffer the wrath of his tongue later.

As the afternoon progressed, the tent became more crowded and we had the not so consummate pleasure of being trapped there for the entire day. The rain never let up. Lots of ladies trying to protect their glamorous expensive headgear in a sweaty overcrowded tent did not make for an enjoyable time as people jostled for pole position. It was like drowning in a sea of politicians. Wannabes had paid vast sums of money for the privilege of rubbing shoulders with these great icons of power for just a few hours. But they believed it would be worth it.

"I was chatting to Minister So and So last week at the races and he was telling me...."

A tale that would be repeated over and over in the following weeks to whoever would listen. The ministers probably weren't enjoying themselves very much either. Some were even spotted creeping out through the back of the tent, into the pouring rain and into the throngs of the free – the men, women and children on the outside. Did any of *them* wish they could turn the clock back as well, I wonder!

27

'In Sickness and in Health'

*S*tress is the bane of all our lives. Work-related stress. Relationship stress. Financial stress. Everywhere we look we see it. Slow down, our bodies shout, but we ignore them. Relax, they scream. Who, me? How can I relax when there is so much going on in my head? Then eventually the body cries halt.

It was now two-and-a-half years since I fled the perceived tranquillity of Donegal and set up life in London. From the very first day I went to find a flat, there had been problems after problems. Four times in those intervening thirty months, I had moved bag and baggage to a different abode, encountering numerous unsavoury characters along the way. Two months after moving into our little house, the landlady from hell resurfaced. She had been silent for almost a year. Once again, she left abusive messages on my answering machine. This time, she threatened to take me to court. She threatened to send the police after me. She filled my life with terror. I could neither sleep nor eat.

Once again, my boss alerted Security at work, who agreed to monitor callers to my office. But who was Security watching out for? I couldn't even describe what she looked like. Was she tall or small? Fat or thin? Blonde or dark? I had never even met this person, as I had rented her flat through the letting agency. I knew what Zorba the Greek looked like and his wife, Mrs Mouskouri. Finally, I looked to my solicitor for help.

"Give her the £500 or forget about her altogether," he advised.

But why should I hand over my hard-earned cash to a landlord who had treated us so badly? And how could I forget about her when she kept threatening me with debt collectors? I was almost afraid to answer my phone. But I was to endure another twelve months of threats before she finally gave up.

Once again, I was living on my nerves. And as for travel stress! British Rail was falling apart. Two years earlier, I could get any number of trains from my local station, which would take me to Victoria in under thirty minutes. I even had the luxury of a seat in those early days. Now I, along with thousands of others, had to stand for increasingly long periods on cold dirty platforms, in the hope that a train might just stop and give us a lift, even if it did take over an hour to complete the same journey. Seats were a thing of the past. In fact on one early morning journey, I stood while a strange man forced his knee between my thighs. One could not afford to be afraid of body contact on these meat wagons. The steam and sweat on wet mornings was overpowering. More so, the heat and the stale perspiration in the evenings were beyond description.

In October, my blood pressure soared beyond its wildest highs, forcing me to attend a GP. I have a pathological fear of this profession and had not been near a doctor – with one obvious exception – for twenty-five years. Now I had no choice.

"I'm sending you for tests," he announced.

My body froze at the dreaded words.

"A twenty-four-hour blood pressure monitor," he explained, "which will take readings every thirty minutes."

Finding my way to the hospital was enough to soar my blood pressure even higher. Then the test results came back. Yes, I was suffering from hypertension. It was official. But not to worry, one tablet per day would soon sort me out. Oh, if only life were that simple. If only I could change my situation? If only I had someone to rely on, to take care of me, to prevent me from getting sick.

Everything had seemed so simple on my wedding day, when the promise to take care of each other was solemnly vowed. It was the most natural thing in the world to look after your partner in sickness and in health. And throughout my marriage there were occasions when it was severely put to the test.

One such occasion began on 13 November 1976. The news I received had not been good. The walls were spinning and the floor rushing up to meet me. Someone pressed a glass into my hand. The suffocating aroma of brandy invaded my nostrils. I gulped it down, choking on its strength. It didn't stop the pounding in my chest or the spinning sensation in my head. I was twenty-six-years-old. I had three small children under the age of five, the youngest still a baby. My husband, sitting across the table from me, had just told me he had a cancerous tumour.

"A testicular tumour," he had said, as the floor gave way beneath me.

It was my daughter's fifth birthday the following day and I had to get ready for her party. I still had to ice the cake. That was my first irrational thought – a vain and desperate attempt to blot out the reality that had just slapped me in the face.

"We have to go to Dublin tomorrow morning to see the specialist," he announced, "and then I'm being admitted to hospital in the afternoon."

He seemed calm, philosophical even.

"Don't worry. It'll be okay," he said for my benefit, but I could see the fear in his eyes.

As the evening wore on, my breathing was becoming ever more difficult. I recalled our conversation the previous evening as we sat together in the local pub having a drink. Earlier he had left the house briefly to 'check out something' in the hospital where he worked.

Later as we sipped our drinks, the conversation became serious.

"We might not be able to do this for very much longer," he said unexpectedly.

"What do you mean?" I had asked, surprised.

His face had looked strained but I put it down to his usual tiredness. He had been doing a lot of on-call work at the time and hadn't been getting much sleep.

"Oh nothing really," he replied.

"We should just watch the money," he continued, trying to cover his tracks. Very unlike him, I thought.

"Just forget I mentioned it."

Now as I sat there, I knew what he had been trying to tell me, but couldn't find the words. He was trying to say, 'I might be dying'.

Instead, the next day he had summoned me, along with some members of his extended family, to the pub. And here we all sat in stunned disbelief. His business at the hospital the previous evening had been to see the surgeon who confirmed his worst fears. Yes, there was a lump. He could not be sure whether it was benign or malignant, but it needed to be operated on the following day. Any delay could prove fatal.

He was twenty-six-years-old, just two years out of medical school, in the prime of his life and the picture of health. There must be some mistake. How could anything be wrong with him? All around me I could hear them questioning him. How long have you had it? What is it exactly? What can be done for it? I listened incredulously, unable to speak. I just wanted to run to the other side of the table and put my arms around him and never let go, but I was unable to move. I was paralysed by fear.

Three short years earlier, I had watched as my father had died an agonising and painful death from pancreatic cancer. His screams, as the nurses tried to inject his then fleshless body with painkillers, were never far from my mind. This was in the era before hospice care and syringe-driver pain control. We had stood by helplessly, as his healthy six-foot, fourteen-stone body shrank to a four-stone skeleton in the frightening space of two months. Was it all happening again? Please, please God, my head screamed. Please. No. Don't do this to him.

Six months previously, a young local man of the same age, with a wife and three young children, had been admitted to hospital with severe stomach pain. One week later he lay dead on the operating theatre of a Dublin hospital. When the surgeon began the operation to investigate the cause of his pain, they found him riddled with cancer. As his wife arrived at the hospital that morning, she was told he had died during the operation. The news had devastated the local community.

That scene was about to be replayed, only this time he and I were the unwilling actors. Jervis Street Private Hospital was the scene for both dramas. More recently, I have stood in the middle of the shopping centre that now occupies the space where the hospital once stood and felt the ghosts blow on the back of my neck. Somehow that afternoon in 1976, we got through the next few hours – possibly aided by large infusions of brandy.

All around me others made arrangements for the care of my children while we planned our journey to Dublin. Birthday party plans went out the window. How do you explain to a five-year-old that her parents cannot be there for her birthday after all? You cannot tell her that her father might possibly die. How could any of us ever bring ourselves to utter those words?

By 10 pm that night, the effects of the brandy had worn off and reality was setting in. I was numb with fear and deathly ill, having drunk neat brandy on an empty stomach, which was now on fire. My head was pounding. Thoughts were racing, bouncing off the sides of my brain like rockets. But the pain in my heart far exceeded the pain in my head.

We had been married for just six short years and now I was going to lose him. How could God do this to us? How could he deprive me of the man I loved so much and deprive my children of their father?

By 5 am I could no longer stay in bed. Strangely enough he slept peacefully beside me. I got up and walked away from the house. I walked for two hours into the countryside, trying to clear my head. I had to be strong for him. I had to help him get through it. What use was I to him if I fell apart? I needed to get hold of positive thoughts. But from where?

The following morning we kissed the children goodbye, leaving them in the care of their maternal grandmother. It was a tearful parting on all sides. What would the next couple of days hold for us all? The six-hour journey from Donegal to Dublin was quiet between us. He became very pensive, naturally.

On arrival in Dublin we went immediately to the clinic of the urologist. His diagnosis was similar to the surgeon in Donegal. The operation had to be performed without delay. It was scheduled for 8 am the following morning.

We went to a pub near Jervis Street and sat in silence. So this was it. The fear in both of us was now at its maximum. We held hands and sat there staring at two full glasses, unable to lift them.

Back at the hospital, the nuns had everything in hand. Thank God for the nursing nuns of old – they certainly brought a different dimension to healthcare. They took us into their gentle arms and soothingly prepared us for the difficult journey ahead. After they had him settled in bed, they set about looking after me. They could see that we were both distraught and worn out after our long drive and the trauma of the previous twenty-four hours.

"We have a private room vacant tonight, if you'd like to stay here," they suggested gently. "You're in no condition to go looking for a hotel."

I burst into tears at their kindness. In those days, I knew no one in Dublin that I could stay with and was dreading the thought of finding a bed for the night. I had even contemplated sneaking into bed with the patient!

That night I headed across O'Connell Street to the Gresham Hotel for some food. It was the only place I was familiar with, having been there with my father years earlier. As I sat in the dining room, the waiter came to my table and looked at me.

"Don't look so worried. It might never happen," he smiled.

My silent reaction to his quip was what did *he* know. It was *already* happening. I was dying inside. It was the first time I had ever heard that expression and in all the millions of times I have heard it since, I can still picture myself sitting at that Gresham table twenty-six years ago. As I forced some morsels of food down my throat, I spoke silently to my father. Please ask God up there to make him okay, I begged.

Early next morning a knock on my door heralded the arrival of my breakfast. On a silver tray lay fresh grapefruit, bacon and eggs, golden toast and hot tea. For a moment I thought I was in heaven. Then I remembered where I was with a sickening pain in my gut. I could not even contemplate eating. It was 7.30 am.

"Your husband is on his way to theatre now. They're starting a bit earlier than planned," the kindly nun said.

"But I need to see him," I protested. "Please let me see him first."

I had so much I needed to say to him, just in case. I had to tell him how much I loved him.

"Don't worry. He's in good hands," she reassured. "Get dressed and come along to the parlour. The surgeon promises to phone you just as soon as he has some news."

In the parlour, in front of a roaring fire, the Matron – also a nun – poured medicinal brandy into a tiny glass.

"Sip this," she urged, as she placed a comforting arm around my shoulder.

We sat there together for two hours sometimes in silence, sometimes in prayer and sometimes talking about my husband and children. Each time the phone rang in the hallway outside, I stiffened. I listened as she spoke in hushed tones to the caller. Each time she came back into the room, I looked up expectantly, searching her face for news. How many other terrified relatives were sitting at that moment in hospitals all over the world, waiting for those words?

At 10.30 am the call came through.

"Marguerite, Mr McLean would like to speak to you."

My body turned to wobbly watery jelly. I pleaded with God once more.

"We're all finished and everything is fine," the surgeon announced. "The laboratory has just confirmed the tumour is benign. We're just sewing him up now, and I will be over to see you shortly. Don't worry, he's going to be all right, thank God. He's a very lucky man."

The tears of joy and relief flooded straight from my heart and out through my eyes, as the Matron and I hugged each other.

Some time later, as I looked down at him with tubes emerging from his body, I knew that I could never have survived without him. We had come so close to the edge. The nightmare of those forty-eight hours is still as vivid today as it was twenty-six years ago. For years afterwards, I worried every time he looked tired or drawn. Today, the disease is far more widely acknowledged and men are continuously advised on self-examination. But in those dark days, it was practically unheard of, and certainly never spoken about in public.

28

Nothing to Declare

The chance to fly all over the world with my husband may never have materialised, but I did manage the odd flight between Stansted and Derry airports, however. Once I began to earn some extra money from my writing, I felt confident enough to splurge a little on occasional trips back to Donegal.

On one particular occasion, the trip proved to be quite emotional for me. I was standing in the check-in queue at the Ryanair desk, my mind a million miles away as usual. This was in the days before I discovered relaxation and meditation exercises for my chattering-monkey mind.

"No Daddy, please don't," a little voice wailed, her gut-wrenching sobs heard all across the concourse.

"Please, I don't want to. I want Mummy," she continued.

"I want to go to Derry, Ireland," a little boy pleaded.

"No Daddy. No. Please, Daddy."

His tiny face was puffed and twisted, as he struggled to free himself from the man's tightly gripping arms.

All around me people stood and watched, or tried not to watch, depending on how concerned they were about not appearing concerned. It was 5.15 pm on a cold wintry March evening, at the end of a long and tiring Friday. As I got to the top of the queue, I could get a better idea of what was taking place. The father, possibly in his mid-thirties, was well dressed and clean shaven. The little girl wore a cute furry coat and knee-length boots, and had her hair tied in a neat ponytail. The little boy was wearing beige cord trousers and a rust-coloured jacket. Aged about eight and four, respectively, I reckoned. Daddy appeared to be trying to convince his children to come and sit down in the adjoining area. Each time he tried to move them, however, they clutched the large suitcase between them, and screamed in terror. My first thought was that perhaps he was trying to abduct them. He had a strong and easily identifiable Derry accent, but the children had a nicely refined London accent. They had mentioned Mummy, but she was nowhere in sight.

Eventually, the Ryanair ground hostess, patrolling the area to deal with mass confusion at check-in desks, approached the small group. I could not hear what she said, but eventually she convinced the children to move with their father to the seating area. The crying and screaming continued unabated, however. As she was walking away from them, I approached her and asked if something could be done to sort out the plight of these unfortunate children, whatever it was.

"Well, they're calling him Daddy, so he must be their father," she replied.

"I'm sure he is their father," I agreed. "But they're obviously in great distress, and I personally cannot stand by and watch this happening."

She said nothing but I continued. "Isn't there someone that can be called, even if it's the airport police?" I asked.

"Yes, I suppose I'd better call the police," she agreed and off she went.

By this time, many people in the queue were beginning to comment uneasily to each other. It was literally impossible to pretend not to notice. Strangely enough though, many people tried their very best to avert their eyes. Meanwhile, the little boy was thumping his tiny fists on the man's chest, and screaming even louder. His older sister sat, still clutching the big suitcase, her pleading sobs failing to penetrate her father's deaf ears.

I'd had enough. I couldn't hold back any longer. Approaching the trio very cautiously, I was unsure of what the man might do to an interfering busybody.

"Hello, I'm going on the flight to Derry as well," I said. "I can't help but notice that your children seem to be terribly distressed about the trip. Is there anything I can do to help?"

He just looked up at me with a blank look on his face and said nothing. He shrugged his shoulders in the direction of his daughter. He appeared somewhat oblivious to the situation around him, or the fact that dozens of people were now watching. I spoke directly to the little girl.

"Do you want to go on the plane to Derry?" I asked.

"Yes, we do, but we're going to miss it," she sobbed.

"Daddy won't put the case on, and we're going to miss the plane," the little boy added.

"Is your Mummy coming as well?" I gently probed.

"No, she didn't want to come, she's at home."

"Where do you live?" I asked.

"In Wandsworth," she replied.

"Are you going to see someone in Derry?" I enquired.

"Yes, my Gran and Grandad, and John and Catherine."

"Well, don't worry, you won't miss the plane," I consoled them.

"But Daddy won't put our case on the desk," she said again.

She was trying her best to stop herself from crying, and was close to biting off her bottom lip in her effort. So I turned my attention back to Daddy.

"The children are worried that you won't check in your suitcase," I smiled.

"Yeah, don't worry. Yeah, there's time. Yeah, it's okay. No problem."

Then the penny dropped. Daddy was drunk. Not drunk as though he had been sitting in the bar all afternoon drinking whiskey or pints of beer. No. It was the kind of drunk that leaves the individual looking to all intents and purposes, as if they are in full control of their body. The kind of drunk that comes about following a three-day drinking binge.

The kind of drunk that means the drinker has now drunk himself into a state where the brain is somewhat comatose. There is an outward appearance of normal function, yet nothing is getting through to the thought processes of the brain.

An old familiar gut-churning feeling was taking place in the pit of my stomach. Daddy was oblivious to the needs or concerns of his children. He was mentally oblivious to the entire situation around him. He was in the land of ME, where no one else matters – a childlike infantile state that had no rules or boundaries. Had he been outwardly drunk and abusive towards his children, he would have been easy to spot. But problem drinkers do not come in neatly defined packages. They often come in nice clothes, with nice smiles. They do not always stagger around hurtling abuse at innocent bystanders. They do not always fall down in a slimy gutter, with vomit spewing from their mouths. No, sometimes they stand up straight, their hair neatly combed, their clothes immaculate, their shoes shining.

"Would it be all right if we all go over and check in your bag, and then the children will be less distressed?" I asked.

"Okay," he replied and stood up.

The children looked relieved for the first time since I had encountered them. But then, Daddy started to walk off in the opposite direction to the check-in desk. Again the cries started.

"No, Daddy, please don't go away again. We'll miss the plane."

"It's okay, Daddy will follow us now," I reassured them.

I caught his eye and pleaded with him to walk to the desk. Two tiny children tried with all their might to heave their huge suitcase up onto the conveyor belt. A man behind us helped them. While they were being checked in, I asked them if they would like to sit beside me on the plane and they readily agreed. This was when they told me their names and their ages; Jenny was seven and her little brother Matthew was nearly four. With one child by each hand, the three of us and

Daddy started to move towards the departure gate. Time was running out and our flight had already been called twice.

"Do you want to come and I'll buy you a drink?" Daddy asked me.

Before I could turn down his offer, Jenny shrieked and Matthew recommenced his crying.

"No, Daddy. You know you're not allowed to drink. Please, Daddy, please come on the plane."

She was pleading with all her heart and looking to me to save them. I looked down at them and saw the faces of little children I loved, twenty-five years earlier. Again that terrifying lurch deep down in my intestines.

"Let's get onto the plane first," I suggested to Daddy.

So he followed meekly behind us like the third child. The two children and I sat by the departure gate for a few minutes.

"Mummy gets very cross with Daddy when he drinks," she explained. "And sometimes they fight."

"Really. Does that happen often?" I queried.

"Yes, a lot. She doesn't like him drinking because he shouts at her. We can hear them when we're in bed and we cry a lot, don't we, Matthew?"

He nodded his little head sadly.

"But we don't tell Mummy and Daddy that we cry, do we, Matthew?"

Once again he shook his little head in response. The tears were brimming onto my eyelids. Just as I believed we were making some progress, across our path strolled the long dark arm of the law.

"Did you call the police about this man?" said the female copper, while the male copper looked on.

I froze. Why did they not just beat me up there and then? Daddy would now do it to me anyway, when he heard that I had turned him in to the Bill.

"No. No. I'm just helping the children," I replied quickly, glaring at her.

So much for the wonderful discreetness of the Old Bill, trundling in complete with size-sixteen hobnail boots. I managed to whisper to the female that Daddy was under the influence.

In hindsight, I should have just left them all to it and gone for my flight, but I couldn't leave the children. I had promised they could come with me to Derry, and I intended to stick to that promise.

"How much have you had to drink, sir?" they queried.

"Fifteen thousand pints," he replied without a care in the world.

Well, did they really think they were going to get an honest answer? I wondered who trained those people anyway.

"I'm sorry, sir, but I must ask you to accompany us to the police station."

Daddy did not appear all that bothered one way or the other. Derry? Police station? What odds? He was only concerned about himself. The children were still clinging to my hands, looking hopefully up at me.

"What about the children?" I asked.

"Oh, don't worry. They'll be looked after."

"By whom?" I asked.

"Temporary foster care," she replied, as though they were stray dogs.

"But couldn't I take them to Derry with me? Their grandparents are waiting there for them at the airport. I'll take the responsibility for them in the meantime."

"No. You can't," she replied, taking them from me and walking towards the exit after Daddy and her male counterpart.

"But how can I find out what is happening to them? Can you give me a phone number to call?"

"Sorry, I have to go."

They walked away into the distance, the little faces of the children looking back over their shoulders at me, possibly wondering why I had let them down on my promise. I was distraught and helpless.

On my arrival in Derry one hour later, I scanned the arrivals area looking for a grandmother and grandfather. But there was no one fitting that description. Perhaps someone had contacted them to say there was no need for them to come to the airport. There would be no darling grandchildren to hug and kiss.

I arrived in Donegal that night with a heavy heart. The image of their pathetic and sad little faces was still clear in my mind. Were Mummy and Daddy so wrapped up in their own problems that they were unable to see what they were doing to these innocent children? Yes, I think they were. Had these children asked to be born or was it their parent's decision? Was Mummy just trying to do the best that she could at the time? Yes, I believe she was. When they are all grown up, I hope they will forgive her. But still, I wonder where are you now, Jenny and Matthew?

29

Breakfast with Bertie

It is a well-known fact that people as seen on television or in the newspaper look totally different when encountered in real life. This would be very true of politicians in particular. I remember years ago when we sat and watched my husband make his first TV appearance, a fifteen-second spot on the *Six o'clock News*. We couldn't believe how different he looked. He was taller, broader and just different, like someone we didn't really know.

This proved to be the same with the many well-known faces I met in person over the years. And, of course, there was always the make-up department. Truly it is amazing how it can transform people on television, especially men. The make-up department can turn pale, spotty, craggy, grumpy men into gods to be worshipped. And the Bunny Carr type of charm schools can turn tongue-tied, muttering, incoherent, unintelligible, cowering, backward politicians into orators on a par with Julius Caesar.

"Friends, Fianna Fáilers, Countrymen, lend me your ear," they bellow from our screens.

But, there is one exception to this rule, where the natural politician shines through – Bertie Ahern. Over the years, many politicians had visited our house in Donegal, mostly small fry, however. But on one particular occasion some years ago, the catch was somewhat larger. Donegal North East was privileged to have the breathtaking excitement of a by-election, sadly following the death of Neil Blaney some months earlier. Fianna Fáil were looking good, and in the weeks leading up to polling day, many of the already elected brethren from throughout the country had come to help out.

On the Saturday morning prior to polling day, Bertie came to town in support of our candidate Cecilia Keaveney. Celia Larkin was with him and earlier in the week I had invited them to stay in our house, if they wished. However, they had opted for the main hotel in town, which was understandable, as it gave Bertie more exposure to potential voters. A bit of a relief for me too, as I had little opportunity to clean the house or even tidy it up, having been so busy with the by-election for the previous three weeks. I had a six-year-old son whose life ambition was to create as much mess as possible. Cleaning up and sorting things out had been put off until after the election.

Throughout that long Saturday, we toured all over the constituency, Bertie, my husband and Cecilia Keaveney, with Celia and myself bringing up the rear. It was a good, fun day with lots of laughs and lots of walking, talking and hand shaking. For some reason, a strong recollection of that particular day was Bertie nearly getting hit by a bus in Buncrana. Thankfully he missed the bus, and vice versa.

Later that night, we all arrived back exhausted at the hotel in Letterkenny, where we dug into some well-earned steaks and a few drinks. Finally we left the company at 2 am after an enjoyable evening.

Next morning at 10.30 am, a telephone bell was ringing somewhere in my head. Ouch, that hurt. My head was splitting. More than two drinks and I usually ended up with a hangover. Even staying up after midnight reduced me to a sleep-deprived wreck. I managed to pull the phone to my ear. I had wanted to let it just ring, but the sound was too painful.

"Bertie and myself will be over at the house in fifteen minutes," my husband announced. "Will you get some breakfast on for us? We're frozen and starving."

For one split second, I wondered, 'Bertie who?' Then I woke up with a bang. It was the Fianna Fáil churchgate collection day and my husband had been gone since before 8 am to do the local church across the road. Jesus Christ, the Taoiseach was coming for breakfast in fifteen minutes and I was still in bed. I knew by instinct there was no food in the house. It had been one of those weeks where we had lived on sandwiches and takeaways. I have known Bertie for quite a few years and I know that he is one of the most easygoing men I have ever met. Well, that's how he comes across anyway. But crikey, even the poor Taoiseach deserves a bit of fresh bread and a drop of milk in his tea.

Thank God the local Spar was just across the road, but then the local church was also within spitting distance. In fact, it was right next door to the shop. So what would I do if Bertie spied me rushing out of the shop with the bacon and sausages under my oxter? I was out of bed and fully dressed in less time than it took to say PANIC! I was just reaching for my purse when the doorbell rang. No, not now, I thought. I'm busy.

I pulled open the door and there stood Celia with two ladies from Bertie's press office, accompanied by one from the local Fianna Fáil ladies committee. Now, if there is one thing worse than having nothing in for the Taoiseach's breakfast, then it is having nothing in for his female entourage. At least with men, one could bluff. But this is where the 'good sitting room' really comes into its own. I ushered them inside, praying that my son had not left his football boots or bicycle in the middle of the floor.

Then I took the local lady aside, and whooshed her out the door while begging her to purchase some fresh brown bread and milk to save my day. As it turned out, they wouldn't have time for a cooked breakfast, Celia informed me. God bless her! She and Bertie already had breakfast at the hotel, so all they needed was a pot of tea to warm them up. The 'boys' would be along shortly. My life was saved!

Bertie arrived with my husband and I made him nice and comfortable in front of the warm gas fire in the sitting-room, with a nice cup of tea in his hand. It turned out that it was only my husband who was starving, having left the house without any breakfast three hours earlier. At least Bertie had the good sense to eat his hotel breakfast! I would feed my husband later, when the guest of honour was on his way back to Dublin.

Bertie is not one to sit for too long in the one place, so after he had warmed up, he headed for the kitchen to get himself a glass of water. He was up and out the sitting-room door before I had a chance to stop him. I shut my eyes tightly and prayed that he wouldn't notice the mess lurking behind the kitchen door. I prayed there was no underwear or shirts drying on the radiators. I held my breath as I went into the room. But there he was, relaxed and happy, sitting at the kitchen table chatting to my son about his toys.

The rest of the party duly followed and so it was that we all ended up sitting around my kitchen table for an hour, in the midst of the mess and the muddle, over numerous more cups of tea. So you see, Bertie is just like the rest of us. He still drinks tea from a mug, still prefers the kitchen to the 'good room'. And just like every other man, he still puts on his trousers one leg at a time. Forever after that, if I heard Bertie was anywhere north of Drumcondra, I went out and did the shopping. Just in case.

30

The Neighbours

As our time in London grew into months and then years, I realised that one positive thing about living in Donegal was that you could be fairly certain, within reason, that your next-door neighbours had come from some civilised planet. However, nothing of the sort could be taken for granted where I lived in Surrey.

Before I bought my house, I had inquired from the vendors as to whether they had encountered any problems with the neighbours on either side. In a terraced property, one has to live in quite close proximity and so it was important to know with whom I was sharing the adjoining walls. I had been reassured that I had nothing to worry about on either side. Well they would say that, wouldn't they? So other than sit in my car and spy on them for a month, I had no option but to take the vendor's word for it. As it turned out, they were being fifty per cent honest. Unfortunately, the other fifty per cent turned out to be the neighbours from hell.

It was 9 pm one Saturday night when I walked into my bedroom, turned on the light, and walked towards the window. As I reached up to close the blinds, horror hit me straight in the face. Flames were leaping ten-feet high in the air, only yards from the window. My God, my back garden was on fire! But no, wait. This was London after all, Surrey, to be more precise – a most beautiful part of England.

However, my humble house stood in one of its less salubrious, rundown and overpopulated areas. The house was on a narrow little street in the middle of a terrace. At the end of the road, on the corner, stood an Indian restaurant, the Gurka Spice. The pungent smell of spices permeated my living room on warm summer mornings the second I opened the windows. Horrible. On the other corner stood a noisy pub. Revellers passed my house each night as they made their intoxicated way home, breaking pieces off the resident's cars as they went. The initial charm I had felt about the area had long disappeared.

On seeing the flames, I recoiled in horror from the bedroom window. I was torn between rushing back downstairs to ring the fire brigade or staying calm and taking a closer look. I opted for the latter. It was totally unbelievable, irresponsible, incomprehensible, and unacceptable. Another GUBU?

Next door, my strange and anonymous neighbours were burning what appeared to be the contents of their house. I use the word anonymous because I had never actually met them, even though I had lived there for over six months. On the other hand, I had actually heard them on many occasions, usually late at night when I was trying to get to sleep. I had no knowledge of their names, nationality, or even marital status. However, I knew from their voices that there was a man, a woman and occasionally two children residing there. Boys, I think. From time to time, I heard them shouting at each other through the walls. Admittedly, I had caught a quick glance at one member of their household. It was a man in his late thirties, I had assumed. He wore his hair in a long ponytail reaching down his back. His arms were tattooed with snakes and vipers. A car sticker on his back window referred to his prowess at kung fu and karate.

That night, they appeared to be having a barbecue but without one essential ingredient – food. In its place was wood, or furniture, to be exact. Through the smoke, I could see two young boys on the flat-roofed extension, shouting with glee as the flames leapt around the back garden. Unfortunately, their garden, like my own, measured roughly six feet by six feet. Nothing divided us but a flimsy three-foot high trellis fence. The trunk of a large mature tree filled most of their side, with its branches overhanging my side of the fence.

Memories of Halloween came flooding back to my mind. DON'T BUILD YOUR BONFIRE CLOSE TO HOUSES OR WOODED AREAS was the official warning from the fire department. These warnings I had issued yearly to my own offsprings as they headed off with their tyres and cardboard boxes. But had my neighbours ever heard of or heeded such warnings?

The fire was at that stage burning closer to the neighbour's fence on the other side of their garden. But then, the wind seemed to change every few minutes. One minute I felt safe, the next terrified. Had I paid my fire insurance? I racked my brains. Yes, I had, thank goodness. Should I go out and ask them to put out the fire? Was I crazy or what? Did I really want to be murdered in my own home on a Saturday night? No, I didn't.

My son was staying overnight at a friend's house, so I was on my own. There would be no one around to identify the murderer. People here did not take kindly to interfering neighbours. This was not Donegal after all. I crept back upstairs again. Oh, my God. They had now carried out from the bowels of their house, three doors, plus what looked like the entire contents of a dining room – broken tables, bits of chairs, carpets.

The flames were leaping into the sky with gay abandon, as the man with the baseball cap and ponytail lifted a large wooden object with his tattooed muscled arms and threw it with all his might into the raging inferno. Sparks lit up the night sky for as far as the eye could see.

"Hurray," shouted the kids on the roof.

Jesus, I mouthed silently. Where in the name of God am I? Am I in hell or what? I could not believe that any person could be so stupid or so thoughtless for the welfare and safety of others, not to mention themselves. I went back downstairs again, and gingerly eased open my kitchen window to hear what they were saying. Would it be, *Brace yourself Bridget, only three more rooms to go now,* or more hopefully *That's it, all finished?*

Immediately, the thick black smoke billowed in through the open window. I slammed it shut. Even in that split second, the smell of burning wood had permeated my home. It brought back some particularly horrifying memories of burning buildings and burning wood. I remembered the torrid stench of burning wood and concrete fifteen years earlier, as I stood with my husband and watched while the bodies of four young children from a local family and the babysitter were carried out of the smouldering remains of what, only the night before, had been their happy home.

It was early one Saturday morning in Donegal and I had been on my way home after dropping one of my sons to football practice. That smell was unforgettable. It clung to everything around it. It hung in the sad air for days, while the entire town of Letterkenny went into mourning.

I also remembered further back to 1971 in Galway, when I stood on our front doorstep with my father, a month before he died. Together we had watched the pall of thick smoke stretch from the city out over Salthill, as part of the main trading area close to Eyre Square burnt to the ground. Once again the intrusive stench hung in the atmosphere for days and weeks, almost up to the time my father died. If he were still alive, would I now be in this horrible position, I asked myself? I doubted it very much. He would never have let this happen to me.

Meanwhile, next door the fire was still burning and I wondered what I was doing in such a place. By 10.30 pm it was burning, less fiercely, thank goodness. In fact, those in charge of it seemed to have disappeared. Perhaps they had gone to the pub to celebrate the disposal of all their rubbish. Perhaps they were thirsty after the intense heat. Perhaps their throats were burning, deservedly. But was it safe to go to bed? Or had they expected me to keep check on the flames? Tomorrow, if I woke up un-burnt alive, I would have an even more unpleasant sight from my bedroom window. The charming sight of a giant black burnt hole in the neighbour's garden would face me each day.

Are people born selfish or do they just grow into it? The irony of it all was that we lived just two hundred yards from the official urban dump, where rubbish disposal was encouraged at no extra charge to the decent responsible citizen.

I thought the fire episode was bad until some weeks later when a dog was introduced to the equation. Not a little dog for their little house and little garden. No. A huge, lunging untrained Labrador pup, about one-year-old. Each morning it was locked in a dark windowless wooden shed in the back garden. It barked and barked throughout the day, until it was released on their return from work each evening.

If I took a day off from the office to work from home, there was no peace and quiet to be enjoyed as the cruelty to the animal continued. The dog was never taken for a walk. Never given any exercise, apart from tearing up the grass in my garden. Well, there was nothing left on their side of the fence, it having all been burnt off weeks earlier.

I toyed with the idea of calling the NSPCA to report the cruelty as I saw it, but could not trust said organisation to protect my identity. Yes, I admit I was terrified and intimidated by my neighbour. And boy did he know that I was afraid of him! Each weekend, I darted furtively in and out to the clothes line, my eyes cast downwards lest I should make eye contact. Well, he was a lot bigger than me!

One day I summoned up all the courage I could muster and pulling myself up to my full height, I enquired politely as to whether he could do anything to repair the fence which his dog had destroyed on its way to my garden each day.

"I'll string some barbed wire along the top of it, if you like," he said menacingly.

Forget it, I thought. It was bad enough living in Colditz without having to look out and see the barbed wire every morning, lest I should forget.

Passers-by were no help either outside my house. Each weekend, a new scratch appeared on my shiny little car, parked on the footpath in the narrow street outside. Apart from scratches, I had busted wing mirrors, dented doors and scratched windows. One Friday night, the wing mirrors of all the cars on the road were attacked with what was undoubtedly a heavy club. All the cars were in the same line of fire, on the same side of the street, away from passing traffic.

The joy at having our own house, a place to call home, was being marred by disruptive neighbours and unruly passers-by. Surrey was beginning to turn very sour.

31

Movers and Shakers

Years ago, when I was a child growing up in Galway, we were extremely privileged to have a government minister living in our midst. In fact, his back garden bordered on our school playground. Gerald Bartley, Minister for Defence, was the honourable man in question. My father used to tell me all about him and great leaders of our country, and one day, while holding his hand out walking in Salthill, he suddenly tightened his grip and pointed excitedly across the road.

"Look, there he is. That's him," he said as the chauffeur-driven Mercedes glided smoothly past us. I felt a rush of adrenaline and a shiver of excitement. Sadly, my father died long before my husband entered this illustrious league of gentlemen and women. But he would have been immensely proud of his son-in-law.

What would he have thought, I wondered, of the idea of his daughter shaking hands and speaking to the great man himself, Charles J. Haughey? Throughout the years I spent visiting Dublin and Leinster House, I had many such meetings with Charlie. But my first occasion was by far the most memorable. We were attending a very oversubscribed Fianna Fáil function in the Burlington Hotel one evening, along with what appeared to be every single Fianna Fáil supporter in the entire country. Thousands of us were swaying in the massive crush to shake the hands of the hierarchy. At that stage, we were but small fry – only a common or garden TD, after all. Not yet singled out for greatness!

We were gathered close to the entrance waiting for the guest of honour, CJ, to arrive. As he made his grand entrance, by some miracle of modern science, my husband and I were thrust directly into his path by those trying to knock us down and trample on us in the pursuit of the golden handshake. CJ recognised my husband, naturally. Well, he was one of his backbenchers after all. The latter took it upon himself to introduce me. Our leader reached out to me, took my trembling hand, cupping it with both of his, and looked deep into my eyes.

"Hello Marguerite, it is such a pleasure to meet you," he purred, in a voice that would have softened steel.

He held my hand and gazed at me for what seemed at least ten minutes, but more likely was only ten seconds by anyone else's watch. As far as he was concerned, I was the only woman in the room at that moment. Possibly the only woman in the universe, actually. I felt it was just he and I. No one else mattered. As he moved on to his next conquest, I floated on a cloud of wonderment. What was it about those soft yet piercing eyes, those warm yet steely hands that could reduce an otherwise sensible member of the female population to a quivering babbling idiot? But then, I was but an innocent raw recruit in those days.

Over the years, I had the privilege of meeting many important figures, both in the world of politics and in many other fields, particularly in sport. I was there the night they invited the swimmer Michelle de Brun to mingle with the ministers. The night they treated her like a princess. The night one had to queue to get the opportunity to shake her hand. What a shame it all turned so sour.

On a more historic note, I was there for the inauguration of the first woman President of Ireland, Mary Robinson, in 1990. Well, to say I was actually in the Great Hall in Dublin Castle was not strictly true. Spouses did not get an invitation to the actual ceremony, a minor detail that my husband had overlooked until the moment we stood in the entrance hall, and I was actually turned away. Never great on minor details, my husband.

So I had two hours or so to kill until the drinks reception in the Castle following the official ceremony. What should I do? Well, this was where the theory I had learned from Monica Barnes in Brussels came into play again. KEEP GOING UNTIL SOMEONE STOPS YOU. Ten minutes later, I was sitting at a desk in a press room somewhere in the bowels of Dublin Castle, speaking by phone to my daughter in London.

More out of curiosity than anything else, I had decided to see how far I would get past security within the Castle. The place was swarming with Gardaí in uniform and Special Branch detectives with their walkie-talkies. It was like Fort Knox in the quadrangle. Yet, I had managed to get past every checkpoint and have the full run of the Castle interior. No one searched me. No one asked me for ID. I'm sure that if I had attempted to get into the actual hall where Mary was being instated, I could have managed that too. However, I did not want to embarrass my husband by causing a commotion. The only reason I rang my daughter was to validate where I actually was. Later, at the reception for the President, I recounted my tale to some eminent politicians. The response was an embarrassed little cough and a nervous laugh.

I was also privileged to be on the scene for the inauguration of Mary McAleese, but this time I didn't bother with the Castle. Been there, done that. Instead, I opted to attend the party in her honour that night. But it was a very enjoyable affair and very informal. It was also the last ever function I was to attend with my husband.

One of the most likeable characters I met on the political scene was the great John Hume from Derry. Some years ago, we were attending a function in the US Ambassador's residence in the Phoenix Park in the company of Jean Kennedy Smith, John Hume and other high-profile individuals. Approximately ten of us were in her private drawing room when news came through of a bomb explosion in the city of London. It was a strange and privileged place to be that night, as gravely serious telephone calls were exchanged in that hushed room between the British Prime Minister, the President of Ireland, the Taoiseach, John Hume, the Secretary of State for Northern Ireland and the US

Ambassador. Later that night, unwinding over drinks back at John's hotel, we listened to one of the funniest and quick-witted storytellers I have ever heard. I hope that his family enjoyed this side of his character as much as I did.

By far my most memorable encounter with the great and the good was meeting Nelson Mandela and his wife Winnie at a reception in Dublin, shortly after his release from Robben Island prison in 1994. This introduction had a really special feel to it. It was like being part of a great moment in history. To be in the presence of a man that would go down in history for generations to come was inspiring. Standing beside him, I felt genuinely and truly honoured to have shaken his hand.

If I ever get the chance to stand for a political party, then I hope it'll be for the Progressive Democrats – if they'd have me! And of all the politicians that I have come across, undoubtedly the one I respect most is Mary Harney. I was privileged to have spent a lot of time in the company of Mary and Co. in the earlier days of my husband's political life. And boy, did we have a laugh. Over the years, we spent many relaxed and entertaining weekends at various secluded cottages and private retreats throughout the country.

One particularly memorable time was when a group of us spent the Whit Bank Holiday at a summerhouse on a tiny private island in Lough Corrib. The house was old and rambling and somewhat in need of repair, but the seclusion it offered to high-profile politicians was invaluable. The owner was charming and laid back, and a wonderful host. The high point was a trip up the river on Sunday afternoon, in a small boat with numerous passengers, many cans of beer and no lifejackets. We were an extremely bad advertisement for safety at sea. Which only goes to show that even politicans have some minor faults.

One New Year's Eve spent in a popular hotel in Connemara was also unforgettable. I vividly recall walking home in the pitch darkness from an afternoon drinks party with Mary, myself and a well-known *Irish Times* journalist falling headlong into a ditch at the side of the narrow country road. What was even funnier was the identity of those who pulled us back out again!

On a more serious note, however, my husband was in the habit of avoiding all social contact with any of his colleagues while I was in Dublin. He seemed determined to convince me that work was his main priority. To this end, he rarely ate in the main dining room in Leinster House with me. I, on the other hand, loved to eat there. It was handy, it was cheap, and it was fascinating. Many of his Fianna Fáil colleagues were busy entertaining themselves, so this was where the PDs came in. Mary or Liz O'Donnell would invite me to join the PD table in the dining room. For anyone not familiar with this particular eatery, each party has more or less their own section. It is not segregated by rails or any such deterrents to keep them apart. Rather it is taken for granted that one dines on a particular side of the room.

Thus, as I moved to the PD section, I was often aware of comments being made by those at opposition tables.

"What's McDaid's wife doing with the PDs?" I might have heard.

The truth was, I was merely enjoying some interesting company, and getting a feel for their politics. Certainly, what I did learn in those years left a lasting impression on me. On all of the occasions that I was in company with Mary Harney, she was always on her own. Not in the sense that there was no one with her, but alone in her heart. She and I had a long lunch together one day and we talked about men, about marriage, about relationships and about loneliness. We were both suffering from it at the time. Mary had a superb job and what many would consider a wonderful lifestyle – out to functions and parties every night, flying off to meetings all over the world, a driver at her beck and call. And a plethora of flunkies to attend to her every need! But she did not have the one thing that she desired most – a loving relationship. A partner that she could go home to after a hard day at the office and seek solace. A partner she could trust. Mary was vulnerable, as many single women in high places are. How could she know if men wanted her for herself or for her power? She was in a difficult position.

It gave me great joy to read in the papers while in London that she had found the man of her dreams. Mary is one of the kindest people I know. She looks after people in her company. She makes sure that no one is left out. She may not have had an easy political ride, but she has always stuck it out. I admire her courage to speak out, even when against popular opinion. I admire the way she continues to hold her head up high despite the many attempts to poke fun at her by the 'artistic geniuses' in some of our newspapers.

Sadly, once my husband received his ministerial portfolio, he forbade me to have anything to do with Mary Harney or the PDs.

"It doesn't look right," he commented. "Stay away from them."

And so, that was more or less the end of that association for the time being. But I think from the radiant look on Mary's face that she is very happy now, as she duly deserves to be.

32

The End of the Line

I suppose when living and working in a big city, one is bound to come across more life and death happenings than one would encounter in a town in Ireland. However, there are certain things to which one never becomes accustomed, no matter where they occur.

The next train due at Platform 2 is the 11.24 service to Victoria, calling at Clapham Junction and Victoria only.

I listened with just half an ear as I stood on the platform of my local station one Friday morning, waiting for my train to London. Equally, I paid very little attention to the sparsely populated platform. After all, it was nearly midday and the serious commuters had long made the daily pilgrimage to work in the city, while I, joyously, had a day off.

I noted a solitary figure at the far end of the platform, slightly out of reach of where the expected short train was due to stop. Still, I paid little heed, as at this particular station one often encounters loners hanging around at odd times during the day. In fact, every time I used the station during off peak hours, I tended to rush through apprehensively, while holding my breath. Always with that slight tinge of fear, as it was quite an isolated spot, as stations go. A young woman had been attacked there one evening not so long before. The police had put up notices asking for witnesses. But parking was free there, which was always a bonus in winter.

At the opposite end of the platform, the ticket clerk was humming contentedly to himself as he dealt with the litter left by the early birds. In my subconscious, I could hear the vibration of the train tracks, which signalled the imminent approach of the train. My thoughts, however, were already four hours ahead of me, at the meeting I was heading for in London.

THUMP.

Have you ever heard the sound of a human body being struck by a moving vehicle? As in a train, for instance? It does not go 'crack' as the bones break. It does not go 'whoosh' as the blood spurts out. No, the word that best describes it is 'thump'. Definitely a dull, sickening thump. Then came the screeching of brakes and the shuddering of the train, as the driver reacted instinctively by trying to bring his engine to a halt. But it was already too late. Far, far too late.

In another part of the world, a small grocer's shop stands on the border between Derry and Donegal. It sells lottery tickets. Over a number of years, this tiny outlet became renowned for the number of winning tickets it had sold. Because of its notoriety, the queues on Saturdays often stretched back over both sides of the border, as we all tried to win our own personal million. People travelled for miles to worship at this lottery shrine. Would a million euro solve all of life's problems? Perhaps it would. Who knows?

Back in England, stands a small British Rail station, Purley. Over the years, it has become like the lottery shop. It has become renowned for being the most successful location at which to end one's life. The best place to throw one's body under the path of an oncoming train. As it turned out, this was now where I was standing.

'An incident on the line' is the terminology used by British Rail guards on such occasions. *We regret that the 14.45 service from Brighton to Victoria will be delayed, due to an incident on the line at Purley.* How often had I listened to such announcements in my time in England? In the local paper it would appear at the bottom of the page eight perhaps. Certainly, no front page headlines deserved MAN KILLED BY TRAIN AT PURLEY STATION. One gets used to it, like most things in life that don't affect us directly.

But this time it *did* affect me.

This time I was *there.*

This time, I was on the platform when he jumped.

Naturally, I swung around instinctively to look.

Instant regret.

I still could not get the picture from the forefront of my mind months later. Not that there was much to see really. No, it was more knowing what was there and visualising it. The reality was that somewhere a few yards from where I stood, under the wheels of a train, lay parts of what minutes earlier had been a human being. I forced my mind away from the gruesome details, and filled it instead with questions. Had I perhaps climbed up the station steps behind him, I wondered. Or maybe it was a woman.

Had I stood behind her at the ticket desk? Was I the last person to see her alive? Why did she want to kill herself anyway? Had she a husband and kids? Was someone making her life a living hell? These are all the strange questions that go through the mind when in shock. Trivial things. But they protect it from the horror of reality. And the sickening reality was that some poor demented soul had chosen to end their life just yards from where I now stood. I just wish I knew their name.

On another occasion travelling to a temping job in Dulwich shortly after I first arrived in London, I got my first real experience of the impact of a motorised vehicle on the human body. It was on a wet misty morning. As I cowered under my umbrella at a busy junction, I heard that unmistakeable THUMP, and then the screeching of brakes. More sickening than either of these sounds was the terrifying scream. The scream of shock, of terror, of pain.

This time my back had not been turned. This time I was watching as the bus pulled up to let the young lady onto the zebra crossing. It was easy to see that the driver of the car behind the bus was impatient. He couldn't see the crossing through the heavy rain, and I watched in horror as he pumped his engine and zoomed out to overtake the bus. In a split second, I saw her fly through the air. Just like a rag doll. I saw her shoes catapulted towards the sky. I saw her handbag sail through the air like it had wings, and land with a thud at my feet, expelling its contents onto the wet ground. I heard the crash as she hit the centre of the road just in front of me. Then SILENCE. Eerie, eerie silence.

Nobody moved. Someone pressed the pause button on the video of life. For what seemed like eternity, we were all frozen in time. Then the silence was broken by a pathetic, gut-freezing whimpering sound. A sort of death rattle perhaps. With this, the video kicked back to 'play' mode. People moved, but seemed uncertain where to move to. If I run to her, people may think I am seeking gory thrills, was my first thought. Strange the way the mind responds, isn't it?

Suddenly a young man standing opposite me sprang into action.

"I'm a doctor. Someone call an ambulance," he shouted, as he rushed towards the unfortunate victim, pulling off his coat, and attempting to cover her. It was like a scene from an American movie. *Trust me, I'm a doctor.* I moved with him, and held my umbrella over her, shielding her from the elements. It seemed like a pathetic gesture. As I knelt close to her on the wet ground, I could see the rain was already washing the blood from her face and hair. I tried hard not to notice the impossible angle at which her right leg lay, limply. I knew that even a Russian gymnast could not achieve that position. Her right arm was twisted behind her back at an equally grotesque angle. Her terrified eyes blinked up at me and I stroked her forehead in an effort to reassure her. She was young and pretty, maybe late twenties, just like my own daughter. As I leaned closer, she made a feeble attempt to call a name. 'Joh, Joh' was all I could decipher as her eyes closed slowly. Was it her husband, I wondered?

As the siren of the ambulance became louder, I glanced up and observed that life had returned to normal on the pavement, with workers going about their journey as usual. Someone else was taking care of the grim sight. Naturally, the traffic had piled up on either side, but would soon be back to normal. To one side, an ashen-faced man was in extreme distress.

"I didn't see her," he proclaimed to anyone who would listen. "She just appeared out of nowhere in front of me."

"I swear I didn't see her," he repeated over and over like a mantra.

Later that morning, I rang the local hospital to enquire about the young woman. I could not get her out of my mind. I needed to know if she was alive.

"Are you a relative?" the Casualty nurse inquired.

"No," I replied, but explained my situation and my involvement in the case.

"Can you just tell me if she made it?" I pleaded.

"Sorry Madam, but we cannot give out that information."

I just wish I knew her name!

The sudden taking of life, deliberate or accidental, is always profoundly distressing and traumatising. It affects us all deeply, the person concerned, their family and friends, their community, even the spectators. For the person involved, the desire to end one's life surely comes with tremendous pain and trauma. The spectre of suicide has darkened many a doorway, not least of all, my own. There were certain events that led to it.

Four weeks before I fled Donegal, the nightmare that had haunted me since 1997 became a reality. As I say, immediately following my husband becoming a Cabinet Minister, he decided that we would lead separate lives. I was superfluous to requirements.

From then on, his affairs became more and more publicised, and the subject of endless gossip and speculation. Finally, I knew that my hopes and dreams would never surface again. They had been smashed beyond retrieval, pulverised into the ground by the person I loved most in the world. I was crushed and broken. It was my final trauma. Too many horrible things had happened in the previous ten years to our family, and I was exhausted from trying to fight for survival.

Such trauma has many stages. At first there is a feeling that everything is okay, because the body possesses a coping mechanism, which takes over on such occasions. One can function without sleep, food, water, alcohol or rest. This period can last for twenty-four hours. Then reality kicks in. And it kicks with a size-sixteen hobnail boot. It kicks so hard that one's stomach and chest area constrict to a degree where even shallow breathing is forced and terribly difficult. In my case, it produced a pain in and around my heart, which nothing could alleviate. It was the kind of pain that tells you that all your hopes and dreams have finally been buried. For years, they had been cut down, built up, cut down and built up again so many times.

His attitude had reduced me to a shell. It left me confused and incapable of thinking for myself. Years later, only after I had received many letters from other women through my newspaper column, I came to realise just what it all meant. Many bullies, of course, are far too cunning to hit or cause any physical injury. However, on the occasions when they do strike in a fit of anger, for some strange reason, it may afford a certain comfort to the victim.

Maybe it is the taste of blood from the lip combined with salty tears entering the mouth that gives a certain reality to the attacks. Or maybe it is some misguided belief that at least one is of some use in his life, even if just providing him with a punch-bag.

It is extremely difficult to fathom how the mind works in these situations. When a victim finds herself on the floor in the corner of the kitchen at 2 am, where her last recollection was of standing on the opposite side of that room, perhaps then she realises that she has actually lost consciousness momentarily from the blow.

Once again the 'why-is-he-doing-this-to-me' factor comes into play. Maybe it is the fact that with mental bullying, she is never sure afterwards if it is imagined or not. The mind is so distorted from trying to protect itself, that it just does not know where it is.

With physical wounds and blood to show, it is almost a relief that she is not going mad after all. When the perpetrator roars like a lion the next morning and tries to convince her that she has imagined the abuse the previous night, then at least she still has the visible scars to prove it. But

still the denial persists. And the survival instinct? *Run. Run. Quickly.*
But where to? Where does she run with small children?

"I know things will get better soon. I know he will change, once he
realises what he's doing to us," she says over and over again. And so she
stays, hoping against hope, and praying.

However, in May 1998, I had run out of hope and prayers. Two days
before I took the hasty decision to run to London, I had sat in my kitchen
with a combination of tablets at the ready. Drugs were easy to come by in
my house. They always had been. In an attempt to induce even a couple
of hours of light sleep at night, I had been swallowing a cocktail of two
sleeping tablets, two pethidine, one valium, three Nurofen™ and a large
vodka. I might as well have been taking M&Ms. Nothing was killing the
pain. Nothing could halt the reel of film circulating behind my eyes,
playing over and over, the horrors of reality. My self-esteem, my pride, my
value of myself as a human being were in the gutter.

I believed that I had only one reason to live – my child was depending
on me. But was I dragging him down with me? Would he not be better
off without me? What use was I to him anymore? A sobbing, broken
wreck who would only ruin his life. I could end it all. I had enough
drugs. In fact, I had enough for both of us. Or would it be better to drive
the car into an oncoming juggernaut? Would that be quicker? Or drive
into the sea? Years earlier, with my two toddlers in the back of the car,
I had narrowly avoided driving into the docks in Galway City, on a dark
wet evening in bad light when the high tide and the roadway seemed
to merge into one. For months afterwards, I had recurring nightmares
of going down under the cold black water, and being unable to save my
babies or myself.

I had tried to talk to the one person whose help and understanding
I craved, but I was informed that I could do as I wished. His only
concern was for me to leave the child alone, and not to harm him. He
would raise him when I was gone.

I formulated a plan in my head. I would arrange for Luke to stay over
at a friend's house on Friday night, and I would take the tablets early

in the evening. This would leave plenty of time for them to do their work while I slept. I would lock the front door from the inside, which would mean that my son could not get in first. It would also mean that my husband would have to get in by the side door, as he was the only one with a key for that door. Then he would find me, in my bed, nicely dressed and ready to go. This would not be an attempt to make him feel guilty at finding me, it would just mean that none of my older children would get there first, as they were all living more than one hundred and fifty miles away.

On the night I had planned the suicide, one of my adult sons rang from Dublin to check on how I was coping. I broke down in tears and confided my plans to him. He was frantic with worry, and unable to contact his father. At the time, we had an answering machine connected to the phone, where the caller's message could be heard as it was being recorded. For five hours into that night, my son called me back, each time I hung up the phone. I begged him to stop calling and trying to talk me out of it, because I just wanted to get it over and done with. The pain was getting more unbearable with every second that passed. I did not want him to change my mind. Each time he called, he begged and pleaded with me to lift the receiver and speak to him.

Somewhere that night, in the murky darkness that had engulfed me, some little light must have shone through. My son reminded me that I had children that loved me very much. He told me that I had an adorable little grandson in England who I had to stay alive for. He assured me that I had friends and family who cared about me. He reminded me too that he and his sister and brothers needed me. Maybe that was it. Maybe I was going to hurt them. How could I hurt them? They were the most important people in the world to me. I pictured them standing beside my grave, grieving. They had been through enough trauma in their young lives since as far back as I could remember. How much more could they take?

Eventually, I made a promise to my son. I promised that I would hang on to life. At that moment, I was barely existing, but I had to cling on.

"Get out of there, Mum," he had said. "You still have plenty of years ahead of you. Get out there and change things for yourself. You can do it. Get away from him and start living your own life. You cannot depend on him for happiness."

So I did not kill myself that night.

33

Lockouts and Leavings

C hristmas 2001 was going to be like no other for me. I looked forward to it with all the excitement and apprehension of a small child. The biggest gift ever was due to be delivered on 25th December – my new grandson. Modern technology had already let us know that it wouldn't be my first granddaughter, but that was of no importance.

Because of the imminent arrival, my daughter and her family opted to remain in Britain for Christmas. They had just moved to their new home in Oxford some weeks earlier and now were looking forward to spending a nice quiet few days together before their new addition. Luke and I flew back to Ireland to spend Christmas in the house in Donegal, as we had done for the previous two years. My husband did not appear to have a problem with that when I spoke to him earlier in November.

However, when we tried to get into the house, it was a different story. He had locked us out. The doors had been fitted with new locks. On enquiring from him, I was told that we could spend the holiday in my older son's rented house, an idea I was none too happy with. Needless to say it had nothing to do with my son, as he made us very welcome and looked forward to having us. But I wanted to be in my own home. I wanted to be able to have my friends around. I wanted to sleep in my own bed, in my own bedroom. I also wanted to be available on the phone for my daughter, should she go into labour. The baby was due on the 25th, but obviously it could arrive any day. There was no phone in my son's house, except for a mobile.

A horrible scene followed the lockout, whereby my husband immediately contacted my daughter. On hearing the news my daughter became quite upset, which was the one thing I didn't want to happen. She had been through a difficult pregnancy and it was terribly important that she be left in peace to give birth. Once again I felt my blood pressure begin to rise and my head begin to ache. My husband could not trust me in the house, it seemed. What was I going to do? Burn it down? Spray graffiti over the walls?

Hours later, through the intercession of family and friends, and a suggestion by me that I might call in the local men in blue, my son and I were allowed entry.

Once inside, we discovered that most doors were locked and the keys hidden. What was he concealing in there? A bomb? In the end, we were able to settle down and enjoy the festivities with our extended family, and I was able to keep in touch with my daughter several times every day. Unable to become part of our Christmas celebrations, my husband moved out to a hotel. I asked him to stay, but he declined.

Over the holidays, I began to seriously consider my position. The lockout was an indication of what he was planning. Obviously, he was intending to move someone else into my house in my place. Over my dead body, I thought. No way. Not the house that I had designed, supervised, decorated myself and furnished. Not my family home. Not the home where my children and grandchildren would come for weekends and for family occasions. No, he had taken enough, but this was where I had to stand up for myself and fight back. I owed that at least to my children. The house was the only thing we had left to show for 30 years of marriage, apart from my wonderful children, of course.

Two months earlier, I had put my house in Britain on the market just to see how much I might actually get for it, should I ever decide to sell. I was totally gobsmacked with the result. The day after it was advertised, there were eight viewers lined up to see it. Its one great advantage was its location within spitting distance of the train station – gold dust for London commuters! Two days later, an offer was made that I could not refuse, and I accepted. Ever so gratifyingly, it was substantially more than I had paid for it two years earlier. But then, I had put a tremendous amount of time and effort into improving it since we had moved in.

So where were we to go? My son had no friends living in our area, but had often mentioned an area on the other side of town, where lots of boys from his school lived. So I went to investigate. But once again, the prices were off-putting. There was no way that I could afford a house there. Then I wondered about getting a flat. But one in a decent area was still way out of my league.

Then, rather surprisingly, I found it. It was on the third floor of a block, mainly occupied by retired people. A beautiful location close to the centre of the village, and it was on the market for £20,000 less than other properties in the area. There must be some catch, I wondered. But, I went to have a look anyway. It had two spacious bedrooms, a large lounge, a decent-sized kitchen and a bathroom with shower. It even had a lift and its own garage. All it actually needed, unfortunately, was new windows, central heating, new kitchen, new carpets, new tiling and complete redecorating throughout. It had been rented for three years and the owner just wanted a quick sale. But it was a bargain.

I got out my calculator and did my sums. If I bought a DIY kitchen and assembled it myself, I could save money. If I did without double-glazing for a while, I could save money. If I bought cheap carpets, I could save money. The form of hot air heating it had would do us for the time being. And the really big one. If I did all the painting, papering and tiling myself, I could save loads on that too. Without hesitation, I put in my offer, and the following day it was accepted. I was quite looking forward to the challenge and spent every spare moment shopping around for the best value in DIY again.

We were due to exchange contracts on 2 December, the day before I flew back to Donegal, and move in on 1 February. But isn't it funny the way things happen sometimes? At lunchtime on the 21st, I got a phone call from my solicitor just as I was about to leave for his office.

"Mrs McDaid, there has been a hold-up with the exchange," he told me. "The person at the top of the chain is not quite ready, so I'm afraid that we'll have to leave it until you come back from Ireland in the New Year. But don't worry. Everything is in order, and we can still complete for February 1st."

I was utterly disappointed, as I had hoped to get the whole thing fixed up and be able to enjoy Christmas. Also I was terrified that my buyer might discover that the damp patches on the living-room walls, which I had gone to great lengths to disguise with mould killer and damp eliminator, were actually worse than they looked. The last thing I needed was for him to pull out of the deal on that score. I did not have a conscience about this, as someone had sold me the same disguised product two years earlier.

On 1 January 2002, my new grandson Dominic made his entry into the world at the John Radcliffe Hospital in Oxford. It was planned to have his hearing tested straightaway, but his parents opted to wait for eight weeks instead. They just wanted to enjoy their baby and put the question of deafness on the back burner for a few weeks. I flew back to Oxford the next day, but foremost in my mind was the question of my home in Donegal.

I had spoken to some friends while I was there, and told them of my indecision. Should I move back to Ireland? Was I strong enough yet? Would it put me right back where I had started four years earlier? How would I feel leaving England? How would I feel living in the same town as my husband and watching him live with another woman? Would I be able to cope with that? How would my young son react to being moved once again?

So I spoke to my son on his own one night. What did he think? How did he feel? It was like two bright lights had come on instantly in his eyes. He jumped from his chair and threw himself on top of me on the couch. He was ecstatic. He would love to come back to his friends and family.

It would mean another new school, but that was no problem to him. He had been attending a local Gaelscoil since he was four, but then had to learn through English while in Britain. Now he was coming back to an all-Irish secondary school. Would it bother him?

"Not at all," he said, "I'll soon pick it up again."

Once again, I thanked God for this amazing child.

Once my daughter got settled back home with her baby, I put my doubts to her. She was totally encouraging. She would love to see me back home in my own house, with my own friends and not in some crummy flat in Britain. If things got bad again, I could always move back to her in Oxford, just like we had in London. But she gave me even more concrete hope.

"Mum, you have changed so much in the last few years," she emphasised. "You are so much stronger now. You won't allow him to beat you down like he did before. You are your own person and you have proved him wrong, so go for it."

So that was it. Maybe I could do it. Maybe I need not let him get control over me again. Maybe I need not let him walk all over me. Maybe it was time I thought of myself. Maybe it would be worth trying just for six months.

"Mum, remember, if it doesn't work out, you can always leave again."

I rang my solicitor with the news. Stanley Zucker and I had built up a wonderful working relationship over the two years since I had first purchased my house in Britain. He was Jewish, in his mid-sixties, just over five-foot tall, rotund and bald. He practised law from a downbeat office in Battersea, and I adored him. He was quick-witted, he was honest and he was totally on the ball. Most important of all, he had twigged my husband straight from the word go. He let him away with nothing. High-ranking, fast-talking politicians, either British or Irish, held no fear for him. He soon put them in their place. I would be sorry to finish my dealings with Mr Zucker.

"Mr Zucker, sell but don't buy," I instructed him by phone.

"Mrs McDaid, I think you are making the right decision," he said frankly. "If I were you, I would go back to Ireland, and claim what is rightfully yours. You have been through enough, so now go back and get a good settlement from your husband. You deserve it."

"Thank you, Mr Zucker."

And so we return to Ireland, ready to face the future. Just as there can be no present without the past, there can be no future without the present. But the future, on the other hand, is a whole new canvas. My future in part became the telling of my story. It is not a story of revenge, of bitterness, of blame. It is written with total honesty for there can be no brushing of truth under the carpet just to make people feel more comfortable or secure. It is a story of life and how the hands are dealt. Some of us turn up four aces, others are not so fortunate. My story is what I was dealt.

Epilogue

Marguerite and Luke returned to Ireland in February 2002 and now reside in the family home in Letterkenny.

On her return, Marguerite founded the Donegal School of Meditation where she teaches weekly classes, in addition to running one-day and weekend seminars throughout the country.

With a store of life experiences, she is studying for a Diploma in Counselling from Queens University Belfast. And with a view to making her own series of programmes, Marguerite is also studying Radio Production.

Though remaining separated from her husband James, she has not lost her firm belief in love and marriage. Undaunted, she believes that one day 'Mr Right' will come along.

"My life," she declares, "is back on track!"